A PLACE TO START

A PLACE TO START

Sylvia Brooks

South Brunswick and New York: A. S. Barnes and Company
London: Thomas Yoseloff Ltd

A. S. Barnes and Co., Inc.
Cranbury, New Jersey 08512

Thomas Yoseloff Ltd
108 New Bond Street
London W1Y OQX, England

ISBN 0-498-07867-1
Printed in the United States of America

CONTENTS

PREFACE

The reader to whom I have written the remarks, instructions, and admonitions contained in this book has become an imagined friend to me, and one whose plight in the ownership of his first horse is an experience shared by many. Much of the material here is concerned with keeping a horse at home; however, the same problems may arise, to some degree, if the horse is cared for by others in a public boarding stable.

I have discussed only some of the ways to go about solving many of the basic problems that may occur when you obtain your own first horse. I do not suggest my solutions to be the only ones. These are just methods that I have found to be helpful and useful with a maximum amount of safety to me, my enthusiastic supporters, and our horses.

Many of the subjects touched upon in this book are personal experiences that have happened to me during almost 36 years of riding and teaching. Some of these instances had very funny endings, but once in a while an injury, which could have been prevented with just a bit more knowledge and thought, occurred to me or my horse.

I was very young (with a big desire to ride), when I met Cornelia Cress of the then Mills College Riding School in Oakland, California. About 12 years later I became acquainted with Barbara Worth Oakford of the

Barbara Worth Stables in Sacramento. These ladies, through their generosity, allowed me to work for them, and in turn they prepared me with a background of equine knowledge that to this day has been unfailing.

In later times I have called upon Mr. B. E. "Joe" Blackwell, Jimmy Williams, Clyde Kennedy, and Jim Black. These men are recognized judges in the AHSA and are considered authorities in their fields of instruction and training. There have been many other people whose abilities have not been noted, but their knowledge has been invaluable.

The original idea of this book came from Gloria McWilliams, and Phyllis Rasmussen was the backbone of the original endeavor. Her hours of reading, correcting, and typing helped to make this possible. Phyllis Hill, with her camera, brought to life so many important points that might have otherwise been ineffective.

The veterinary pages were made with the guidance of Doctor William R. Nissen, D.V.M., who has always taken care of our horses and kindly did so again in this chapter.

To all of these friends I am very grateful and truly appreciative of their help and advice.

Sylvia Brooks

A PLACE TO START

1.

BUYING A HORSE

The act of acquiring a horse is similar to many major events in our lives. When it is finally possible to select a horse for your very own you will find it very tempting to fall in love with the first available on the theory that if you reject this one, circumstances might change and you might not be able to get a horse at all. There are many wonderful horses in the world, and as strange as it may seem horses that will please you as much or more than this first "perfect" one. It may be a good idea to look again for here are several questions you might ask yourself before coming to a final decision.

First: Someone—you or your father or your mother—is going to spend good money for this horse. Will you get full value?

Second: Does this horse suit you? Will he be able to take you to the places you will want to go? Will you be able to do just what you've always wanted to do with a horse?

Third: How old is this horse? Does he have the disposition and temperament that you want? His disposition and temperament, whether he is two or 20, can make all the difference in the world when it comes right down to the real enjoyment of owning a horse.

I find that so often the inexperienced parent feels that "the child and colt should grow together." The acquisition of a "green" or unbroken colt for a completely novice child and family can only lead to disaster. Without the guidance and training of an experienced horseman both the child and colt can only go the wrong way.

It is my considered opinion that an inexperienced family can learn horsemanship more readily from a mature, well-behaved horse—a horse whose experience has taught him to move slowly and deliberately rather than an adolescent who has not learned to protect himself and his owner or rider from hazard or injury.

Fourth: Has this horse received the education required to fit him for the purpose that you intend to use him? This training may be quite simple if you wish to ride him in rural country with no hazardous obstacles. A higher degree of training is necessary if you intend to ride in large parades or jump large ditches and fences in horse shows. An untrained horse will not be able to perform well and will require capable instruction. Competent training by a qualified person will be an expense that must be charged to the cost of the horse. A horse already trained may cost less in the long run than one that needs training. A badly trained horse with undesirable habits is seldom a bargain. Long periods of constant correction may reclaim this horse, but there is the chance that his vices are chronic and may never be overcome.

Take a responsible disinterested party along to voice an opinion and to help you answer these questions. If you are fortunate enough to have a veterinarian friend who will also give you advice on the soundness of this horse you are ahead of the game. Possibly you can ask a local professional horseman for his advice and then have the animal checked for soundness by a veterinarian. In any case, seek the advice and help of someone who has had recent experience with the horses in the area.

You now own a horse—a wondrous, sometimes erratic, sometimes quiet, unknown quantity of grandeur. Get to understand something about this animal. Spend time watching your horse when he is loose in the pasture. Getting acquainted with how a normal horse acts when he is free will give you a standard of comparison when you observe that he does not move or act normally. Prompt observation that he is not acting right will permit you to correct this condition before it becomes more serious.

2.

HANDLING YOUR HORSE

Horses enjoy the freedom of a small field or a corral, so protect their freedom by having the enclosing fence in good repair. If it is possible, avoid keeping your horse in an area surrounded with barbed wire. A horse that has become caught in wire will struggle to escape and in so doing will almost instantly inflict a bad cut upon himself. Enough cannot be said about the seriousness of wire cuts. They may result in many and costly trips by the veterinarian, weeks and maybe months of caring for a crippled horse, and after all this the possibility of a lame horse for a long period of time.

Here we are referring to the usual small lot or corral in which many "at home" horses are kept. In large pastures a horse has plenty of room to roam and usually will stay away from the fence line.

When your horse is in his pasture or even his stall, you will want to catch him to prepare him for a ride. Enter the enclosure and *close* the gate behind you to prevent his escape. When catching loose horses, go prepared with a halter and lead rope and a bucket or pan of grain. In an emergency your belt will help, but do not try to hold on to a loose horse with just your hands. If you do grasp the animal by his head or neck in your attempt to restrain him you will find out very quickly just how strong he really is. Just with the quick thrust or toss of his head he can send you spinning away. Your face can be badly bruised and your backside severely slapped by your sudden arrival upon the ground.

When turning a new horse into a group of horses that have been together, watch them for awhile. Some horses, just as some people, don't get along well with each other. A horse with this attitude toward the others can cause serious trouble with his biting and kicking. However, you can help this situation, for when you feed hay, place many piles far apart. This method will allow the horses to eat at a distance from one another. You soon will find it amazing how a group or herd of horses will select their own friends and leaders. Their social adjustment to life might suggest a better way for humans to live.

Do not leave halters or ropes on your horses when you turn them loose in a pasture. Horses have a way of catching their halters on a protruding tree limb or on a fence. When a horse finds himself caught, his first instinct is to get free. He will plunge and then pull back, breaking your halter, the tree limb, or the fence; or failing in his effort to escape, he will remain caught until someone finds him. If he is out in a large pasture, a day or more can go by that he is without food or water.

If horses are used to being fed oats from a bucket or sack they usually will come to you so do not try to outrun them. Try to trap them quietly in a corner of the fence and then go to the head. Even when you have your rope on he may still pull away from you. Turn him loose and try again. If there are several horses in the pasture they all will come to you when they spot the feed bucket, and you may suddenly find yourself quite surrounded. *Watch out!* These horses, in their enthusiasm to reach the feed may bite and kick at one another, quite possibly injuring you. Catch your horse as quickly and quietly as possible and watch where you are going as you walk away from the others.

HALTERS AND LEAD ROPES

When you wish to move your horse from one place to another, for example from his stall into the corral, carefully

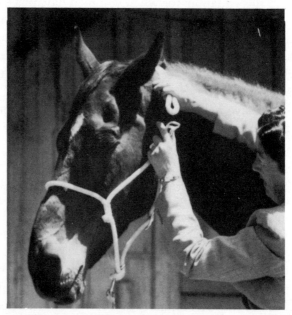

Before starting out with your halter and rope in hand, know how to correctly put this halter on your horse's head. The buckle or loop for fastening is always on the left side. The horse's nose goes into the fixed loop with the longer end passing up and behind the right ear. Bring this end over the head and fasten it on the left side just below the horse's left ear.

The lead rope should be eight to ten feet in length. It should be tied or snapped to the ring on the halter under the horse's lower jaw. The lead rope is held in your right hand. The extra length is held in your left hand, off the ground, away from your feet and your horse's feet. Do **not** wrap the lead around your hand, arm, waist, neck, or leg. **Hold** it in your hand. When leading your horse have the halter on his head and your lead rope snapped or tied to the halter and held in your right hand.

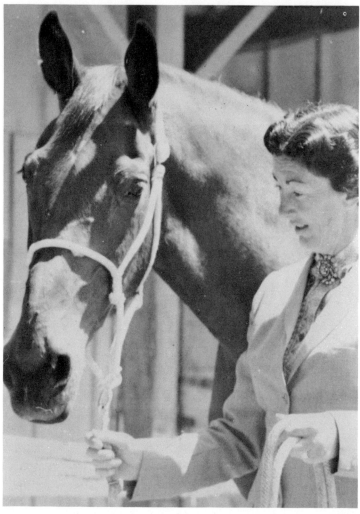

Get into the habit of leading this way. When you lead
a horse with just your hand on his halter you increase
your chance of a very sore hand. As your horse pulls
away from you, your hand can get a severe cut just from
the strength of his pull.

lead him through all barn doors or gates that are opened as wide as possible. Give him room to pass through without striking his hips or catching a stirrup on the gate posts. At the very start make your horse follow you through all openings. Don't let him get into the habit of dashing by you into his stall or into his field. Teach him by jerking the lead rope sharply when he wants to crowd past you. By barging ahead he can knock you into the gate post or the wall of the stall. Don't get into the habit of turning the horse loose to enter gates or barn doors. Horses quickly learn to "dive" through these openings and can injure themselves by striking a hip on the gate or sidewall.

When you lead your horse through the gate into his pasture be careful as you turn him loose. As you reach up to remove the halter from his head, do so quietly. As the halter slips off do not yell or stamp your feet to encourage him to race away from you. There is a great possibility that in the first leap for freedom the animal will kick back right in the direction that you are standing. As the horse gallops away you can be thankful that his high-flying heels missed you this time.

TIEING UP HORSES

A horse, by nature, is a creature of flight. This statement alone should suggest the possible turn of events. When your horse becomes frightened his first thought is to flee. His first attempt toward freedom is usually to the rear with a mighty pull. There will be a brief contest between him and his restraining tie as he seeks to escape in flight.

As a general rule you will not be able to tie a horse so securely that he cannot break away. Tie him so that when he does pull away he will do the least possible damage to himself and all surrounding horses and riders. If you do not have a halter but just a lead rope, tie the rope around the horse's neck, behind his ears, with a bowline knot only. Learn to make and use this knot. It will not tighten around your horse's neck and strangle him as he pulls back.

I prefer to tie a horse with the halter on his head and the lead rope to the fence. When tieing your horse to a post, fence, or barn, use a slip knot only (refer to Chapter 7 for tieing to trees). The slip knot is the one knot that you can quickly pull loose should your horse become entangled in his rope. Getting to your horse and being able to free him immediately when trouble starts can save a lot of broken equipment.

KNOTS TO USE

A horse is not like an automobile; you don't just park it, remove the keys, and walk away, knowing that it will be there when you return. When you have tied (parked) your horse you had better check several items thoroughly before "removing the keys."

1. Is your horse comparatively safe where you have left him tied?
2. Has he been tied where he can get into the least possible trouble?
3. Is he tied where the least possible trouble can come to him?

A horse that is tied too short—when finding just the natural movements of his head severely limited—will feel trapped and struggle for more freedom.

The halter that you use on the horse's head, over the

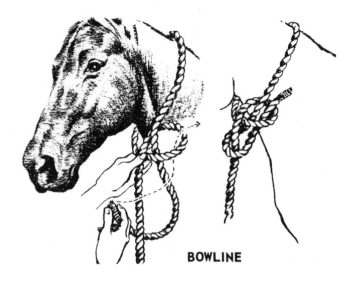

BOWLINE

bridle, must be large enough to slip on easily. It should not confine or pull on the reins or bit. The reins should rest lightly in the halter.

If your horse is wearing a martingale or breast collar, the strap just in front of the withers will slip toward his ears when he lowers his head. With my western saddle I run the rope strap through the collar strap and then over the saddle horn. With the English saddle I run a piece of cotton string through the pommel "D" ring and around the collar loop. A collar piece that can slip behind the horse's ears may cause him to toss his head, thus breaking the collar strap.

The practice of tieing up horses by the bridle reins is done by some people. I feel that tieing your horse by the bridle reins, at best, is very poor. But, if you must, I would suggest that when you are using tied or rawhide reins just lay the reins several times over the fence. This will enable the horse to pull the reins free and have them dragging on the ground in front of him. However, you have saved your bridle, reins, and fence from being broken. If you get to your horse quickly and quietly you may also prevent more broken equipment by picking up the reins. The pos-

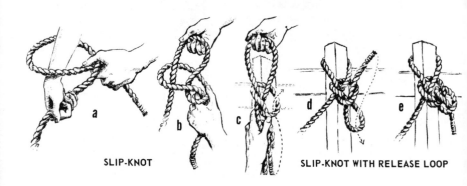

SLIP-KNOT   SLIP-KNOT WITH RELEASE LOOP

sibility of recovering your horse with the bridle reins in good order is greater than if you had tied up hard and fast.

When using split reins, lay the right rein several times around the saddle horn and tie up with the left rein. If your horse has become frightened and pulled away you will find he was able to break just one rein. You will still have the complete right rein to fasten to the left side of your bit and you can continue your ride home.

If I find it necessary to tie my horse when I'm riding with a snaffle bridle I fix my reins in this manner. I unbuckle the reins and loop the right rein lightly around the horse's neck behind his ears. To keep the right rein in place I knot it loosely to the throat latch. Now you can lay the left rein several times over the fence and your horse is tied up.

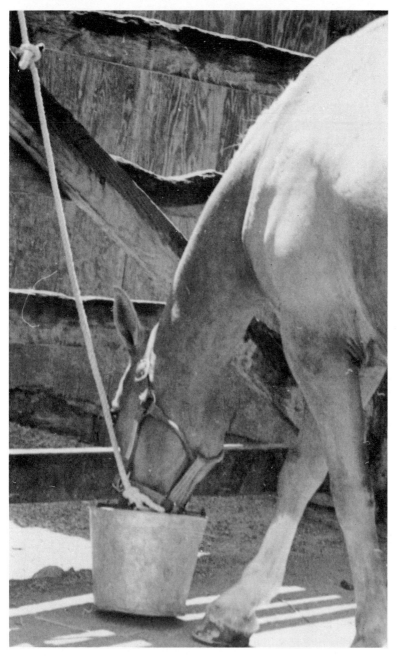

From the fence to the halter a good rule of thumb for the proper length of rope is about three feet. Allow enough rope so the horse has some freedom of his head but not enough length of rope to permit him to get his front foot over the rope when eating off of the ground.

Holding or tieing your horse out in an open field so that he may have an extra feed of new spring grass isn't the best idea. When you are at the end of a 10- or 12-foot rope with him at the other end things can happen quickly. If he becomes frightened and whirls away you may find yourself directly behind his heels in danger of being

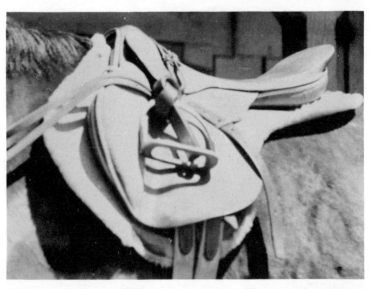

When riding my English saddle I like to tie up my horse in this manner. Run the stirrup irons up to the stirrup bar on the inside stirrup leather. Place the reins under the stirrup irons on both sides. With your halter on over the bridle you can now tie your horse and he will be comparatively safe. He cannot get his head down to break the bridle reins that otherwise would fall over his ears. If you wish to lead your horse take the reins out from under the stirrup.

kicked. Standing in front of the animal could knock you down as the horse plunges by. You have very little control of your horse when there is a long rope between you.

If a horse is tied or staked out, and he is frightened, he can become entangled in his own rope and cause injury to himself. It really isn't worth it. A long stake out rope that has wrapped around your horse's leg will cause a severe rope burn, which requires care and medication to prevent lameness and a possible scar.

MISFEEDING

These extra treats that we humans will offer our horses can cause trouble.

The green grass in the spring seems like a delightful change for horses that have been kept in a barn and fed hay all winter. To let a horse have all the grass he wishes on the first day out will make him sick, because it is too sudden a change in his diet. Start by letting him eat for about 20 or 30 minutes at first and gradually increase to an hour or two in several days. Let his system become used to the new feed now available.

Many people enjoy giving a treat of cube sugar or a carrot by hand to their horse. We feel that the horse will get the same enjoyment from the gift if it is placed in his feed box. If you do allow your horse to take food from your hand be sure to keep the hand flat and fingers stiff. Small children should NOT be allowed to feed horses this way. A three- or four-year-old child has a very small hand and his little fingers just curl up.

Some folks will allow their horses to drink coke or beer from a glass bottle. What this proves I do not know, for neither liquid does the animal a bit of good. The glass bottle can get broken in the horse's mouth, and I'm sure you don't want to fish the glass chips out of his mouth.

LAWN CLIPPINGS

You will find that so many horse areas are now right next to a new housing development. The residents in their new homes work hard to maintain the good appearance. Keeping the new lawn cut each week is a regular chore, and disposing of these lawn clippings over the fence into your horse's lot seems to them the proper thing to do. For your horse's health you must remove these clippings immediately. It is the rapid fermentation and bacteria growth in the cut grass that will cause your horse distress. Cut grass left in a pile cannot get exposure to the air and light so it can dry and cure in the sun. Try to meet your new neighbors, explain this situation to them, and possibly prevent the tossing of greens into your horse's lot.

3.

STABLE MANAGEMENT

Many centuries ago man took the horse's freedom from him and made him a beast of burden. In return for the loss of freedom man owes this animal the best care and feed that he can provide.

While working in the stable—feeding, grooming, or cleaning—remember that a horse is easily startled by a strange noise or movement that he had not anticipated. When working around your horse move at an even tempo and be sure he is aware of your presence. Always let a horse know when you are coming up behind him. Some people whistle or talk gently when they are around stock.

Horses are grazing animals. When they are free they will crop at the available feed about 18 to 20 hours in a given day. We feel that the more often food is available the better horses will do on the feed. The more frequent feeding, which a horse will clean up, is a better way.

It is so apparent that many new horse owners will think only of the fun of getting on the horse's back and going for a ride. They never seem to realize that when they obtain a horse for their pleasure they in turn must provide him with clean living quarters, good feed, and plenty of fresh water for his comfort.

PARTS OF THE HORSE

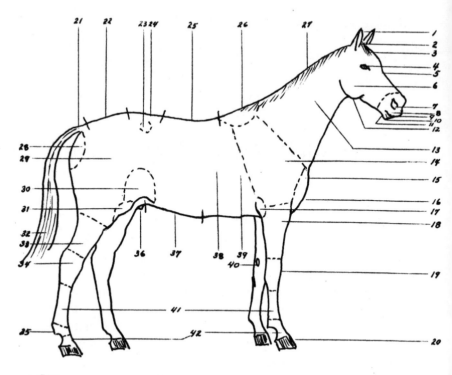

1- EAR	13- NECK	25- BACK	38- BARREL
2- POLL	14- SHOULDER	26- WITHERS	39- GIRTH
3- FOREHEAD	15- POINT OF SHOULDER	27- CREST	40- CHESTNUT
4- EYE	16- CHEST	28- BUTTOCK	41- CANNON
5- FACE	17- ELBOW	29- THIGH	42- PASTERN
6- CHEEK	18- FOREARM	30- FLANK	
7- NOSTRIL	19- KNEE	31- STIFLE	
8- MUZZLE	20- HOOF	32- TAIL	
9- UPPER LIP	21- DOCK	33- GASKIN	
10 LOWER LIP	22- RUMP	34- HOCK	
11- CHIN	23- POINT OF HIP	35- FETLOCK	
12- THROAT LATCH	24- LOIN	36- SHEATH	
		37- ABDOMEN	

Feed at regular time and convenient intervals. Make it easy on yourself and start by feeding at a definite time in the morning and afternoon, but regularly at these times.

When a horse is confined to just a stall or corral he may very quickly become bored. His only change of pace, so to speak, is feeding time, and he will count on being fed at these definite times each day. When the time varies from day to day often his disposition will change, and usually for the worse. His general health and condition will become poor and his coat listless. If you cannot care properly for your animal, the kindest thing you can do is to sell or even give him to a person who will.

Carry the hay in your arms when feeding your horse. Don't use a pitchfork to throw hay into the manger at the horse's head. Hay can be fed from the ground, but be sure the ground is clean (i.e. free of droppings etc.). Store your hay where dogs cannot wet on it, chickens and other fowl cannot spoil it, and children do not play on it. Hay that has been improperly cared for will lose its appeal to the horse and will be wasted. Check your baled hay for mold by breaking the bales. Heat, discoloration, and a strong musty smell are signs of spoiled hay, which should not be fed to horses. Horses do not seem to know that spoiled hay will make them sick so you must be very observant as you give yours his hay. Hay that does not look or smell just right had best not be fed to your horse.

If you store your hay in a stack be sure that it is well covered with a tarp or plastic before the first fall rains come, as hay that has been rained upon will become moldy and unsuitable.

It is almost impossible to price the cost of feed in different parts of the country and from season to season. A poor crop year will send hay prices sky-high. One thing we do know, no attempt should be made to economize at the expense of quality. Generally one and a half pounds of hay per hundred pounds of horse per day will be adequate. More than this will usually be wasted. Feed just what your horse will clean up each time. The average horse will weigh about 1200 pounds, so he will eat some 550 pounds of hay per month or about three and a half tons a year.

In your feeding program, local conditions will play a large part, as some crops will do better in your area than others. The appearance of hay is most important. It should be a good green color, clean and bright (not dusty and dry), and should smell sweet. Any musty smelling, hot, or damp bales should be rejected. If storage permits, it is far more economical to buy hay in quantity. In the summer or early fall, when hay is usually cheapest, obtain three or four tons—a year's supply for one horse.

The grain ration will vary with the horse's weight and the amount of work he does. Oats are the standard grain feed and are best rolled, being more easily digested. Barley is fed a great deal and is usually cheaper and has more food value than oats. Corn is fattening and should be fed lightly, especially to horses that are not used to it.

Bran is a laxative that is used in a small amount—1 or 2 handfuls—and mixed in the grain. A bran mash is made by adding boiling water to the bran, then covering and allowing to steam until cool.

If you are working your horse regularly, possibly a feed supplement will be necessary. Your local feed store will carry several very good conditioners to add to the feed. Read the instructions carefully and use accordingly.

A possible feeding schedule:

A.M.—minimum hay and light grain

Noon—minimum grain

Late P.M.—minimum hay feed

Later in evening—larger feed of hay to last most of
the night.

If you are going to ride your horse, feed hay when you
return. Do not feed any grain to an overheated horse, only
hay until he is cool.

Walk-in stalls with an overhead shelter will keep the
horse's feed dry as he eats. If you cannot build this type
of shelter, construct a "crib," which can be made by build-
ing a trough about two feet wide and three feet high.
Over this build just enough shelter to keep the rain off of
the feed. If you place upright 2x4's about a foot apart,
your horse can put his head in to eat the feed. A horse
will do very well left out in all weather, but you must
provide some shelter for him. By keeping his feed edible
and dry he will stay in good condition to withstand the
elements to greater advantage.

To provide the needed salt in a horse's diet, use block
salt on the ground where it is available to the horse. In
hot weather, because of heavy sweating, be sure salt is
available at all times.

A water tub, bucket, or trough should be large enough
for a full day's supply and should be secured in position
so that it cannot be overturned. Do not fasten it permanently, however, because the bucket should be emptied
and cleaned two or three times a week. The carry-over
from the horse's feed to his bucket will leave enough material in the water to spoil. Be sure that the bucket is in
good repair and does not have sharp projections that might
cut the horse.

Your horse will need a great deal of water—five to 15
gallons a day depending on the weather. If water is not

available to the horse, he should be taken to water three or four times a day and allowed to have his fill each time. Automatic water bowls are a great timesaver; the initial expense is relatively high but they will pay for themselves in man hours saved.

A hot horse should not be watered and allowed to stand. However, he can be allowed to drink a sip or two at a time while he is kept moving until thoroughly cool, after which time he can be returned to his stall or corral.

Feed bags are easy to make from gunny sacks and are handy to have for feeding grain or oats. Cut the sack in half and stitch or hem the open sides. Attach a piece of twine or rawhide to each side, forming a loop that will pass over the horse's ears. Horses learn quickly to put their noses into the sack and eat all the grain without much waste. Those that have been fed from grain sacks come readily at the sight of the feed sack. When removing the twine or rawhide from behind the ears, watch that the horse doesn't throw up his head for that last mouthful of grain and strike you.

If you wish to provide bedding in the stall for your horse to lay upon, clean pine shavings are possibly the best. Redwood shavings may cause skin sores and some infection for they seem to work into the horse's hide. If you are bedding your horse with shavings in his stall, this must be cleaned out regularly—*once a day!* The droppings are picked out and all the wet shavings removed. Protect the bedding supply against foul weather by storing it in a shed or covering the stack with a tarp. After cleaning the stall, a small amount of lime, obtainable in sacks from a builder's supply house, may be sprinkled on the wet earth to prevent a septic condition that will in turn prevent odors in the stall. Keep the lime supply out of reach of the animals. Should your horse break into the sack, the moisture from his nostrils and lips coming into contact with the lime could burn his mouth and nose. We store the lime in a covered garbage can.

There are several types of bedding straw—wheat, oats, or rye—and it too should be clean and bright. You can usually figure on using five small bales of straw per stall per week. We have used peat moss, which has great absorbent qualities and keeps down odor, but it is rather expensive. Disposing of your soiled bedding must be considered. Straw, for example, soon will make a large pile to remove. An ad in your local paper may help you contact a truck gardener who will remove the manure. Peat moss in this respect is a welcome addition to any gardener.

TIE OR STRAIGHT STALLS

Under some stable conditions the use of tie or straight stalls is the right answer. Keeping horses in tie stalls in the barn or in an outside shelter often will minimize construction costs. Horses that are exercised several hours each day will do very well in this type of stall.

Tie stalls are easier to clean and maintain. Feed and water can be easily changed from the front. A horse that is kept in a tie stall will always find his own place, even if the rest of the barn is empty. Our horses walk quietly into their own stall and stand easily until needed. At night we never leave the barn until the rope or "butt" chains have been fastened behind each horse. These ropes are heavy cotton or chain fastened securely to the right rear post and, with a large snap, to the left rear post. These ropes are about three and one-half feet from the floor and help to keep a horse from pulling back out of his stall. Should the tie rope in the manger come untied the horse may turn around but will remain in the stall facing outward until morning. In outside shelters each horse has his own stall in which to eat and drink. These outside stalls also give protection from the hot sun and poor weather in the winter.

In all past reading you may have noted that a great deal of emphasis has been stressed in providing shelter or protection from the elements for your horse. I am referring to so many horses that are kept confined in a small lot or corral. In these conditions the area is too small for them to find natural shelter from the heavy wind and rain, and the ground shortly becomes a bog from the water. Horses rest standing on their feet, but after a prolonged period of standing they must lie down. A horse will seek a dry, well-drained, or sandy spot in which to rest. When a horse is kept confined, these areas for dry rest and feed are not available to him, so they must be provided by you.

Horses that are kept in large pastures—200 acres or more—can seek and find the natural shelter that Mother Nature has provided for the animals on the land.

FLY CONTROL

Fly control is a most important factor wherever animals are kept. If your horse barn is in or near a residential district, and just about what area nowadays isn't, you must control the fly population so your neighbors won't complain that your horse is creating a nuisance. When the Health Department officer or Fly Abatement people check on your barn they will find that you are maintaining and using the proper fly control measures.

Bulletins on fly control are available in each county from the Health Department. I have used just a few important points from the Alameda County Health Department bulletin.

The life cycle of the common fly starts with the egg stage, from which in three or more days about 1000 eggs may be deposited. The larva stage, which lasts from three to 75 days, will follow. The larvae are worm-like and they feed in or on moist organic matter or even in water with a high organic content. Then comes the pupal stage, which may last from a few days to a month and is the time required for the development of the larval to the adult form. The complete life cycle may last from six to 45 days.

Control all organic material in which flies develop. Specifically this means providing good drainage so that manure and spilled feed does not become wet. Have faucets and water troughs that do not leak. All buildings and corrals should be accessible so that manure can be hauled away as needed, and there must be a complete removal of all organic material from the premises every seven days. General control measures are sanitation, and chemical control is in the form of sprays, dusters, aerosol mists, and baits.

In all cases proper sanitation will be more important than ever. Precautions should be taken with all insecticides. Obtain your fly information from your local "Fly Man" and be a good horse neighbor.

BOTS (GADFLY EGGS)

While we are on the subject of flies I think something should be said here regarding bots. Bots are the larvae of the gadfly. This fly will lay its eggs during August and

September on the skin of horses. The adult gadfly is yellowish-brown in color, hairy, and parasitic. The female will typically lay her eggs on the front of the horse in areas that he can reach with his tongue. The eggs will remain unhatched if the horse does not lick the infested area. When entering the horse's mouth, the eggs penetrate the mucous membrane of the gum, lips, and tongue and gradually wander down into the pharynx. The larvae will remain in the membrane of the pharynx for a short time living on blood but will soon pass on to the stomach where the rest of the life cycle is spent.

When so many horses are allowed out in a pasture or corral the appearance of the bot larva should be watched for. The eggs will be yellowish-white in color and found around the fetlocks and cannon bone of the front legs. The stomach and chest are also vulnerable to host the eggs.

The best means of prevention is to keep your horse away from pasture and in the stall at this time. However, this is not practical or possible in many cases.

When the bot eggs appear we remove them with a razor blade. Using the blade in the direction of the hair the eggs can be shaved off. I feel that the immediate observance and removal of the eggs is a must for the general good condition and health of your horse. Should you obtain a horse that has been in pasture and become badly infested with the bot fly eggs, the advice of a veterinarian should be sought.

GROOMING

Take pride in your horse's appearance. Keep his coat clean, free of mud and manure stains, and his mane and tail combed and pulled neatly. Horsemen will judge you by the condition of your animal.

Before riding, clean your horse, particularly brush his back. Remove all old sweat, dirt, mud, stickers, and hay before putting on the saddle. When grooming your horse begin on the left side and work from the ears to the tail. For grooming we find that the following basic tools are needed:

1. Curry Comb, metal or rubber, round or square. The round rubber curry comb fits best in my hand. It is used in a circular motion on the body to loosen the dirt in the horse's hide.

2. Corn or stiff bristle brush to remove the dirt. This brush will help to straighten out the mane and tail. Mud and manure can be removed from the hocks and knees with the stiff brush, but proceed in a firm and gentle stroke.

3. Finishing or soft bristle brush to remove the fine particles of dust left on the coat. This soft brush is the one to use on your horse's head and face.

4. Additional pieces of grooming equipment are sponge, mane comb, hoof pick, and a wire brush.

Brushes should be kept in some kind of box with the bristles facing up so they will last longer and be easier to find. Finish by carefully checking and cleaning each foot with the hoof pick.

If your horse's hocks or knees have become stained from manure, warm water and mild detergent or castille soap on a sponge will help. Squeeze the soap into the sponge and wipe the hocks in a downward motion. After the stain has been removed, rinse thoroughly to remove any remaining soap.

With a clean sponge that has been dampened in clean

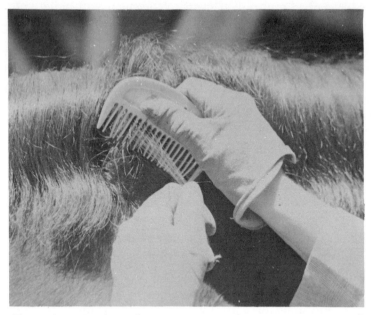

To make your horse's mane even and neat you may pull the longest hair out. With your mane comb in your right hand, firmly grasp a few of the longest strands of hair in your thumb and forefinger of the left hand.

water, wipe around your horse's eyes and muzzle to remove the dried moisture and dirt. Carefully wipe inside his nostrils. Remove the dirt from the dock (under his tail) in this manner.

A light flannel or velveteen cloth used on the body in the direction of the hair growth will remove small particles of dust and add a finishing luster to your horse's coat. Old bath towels are excellent for drying the long hair on the shoulders and loins in the winter when your horse has a heavy winter coat.

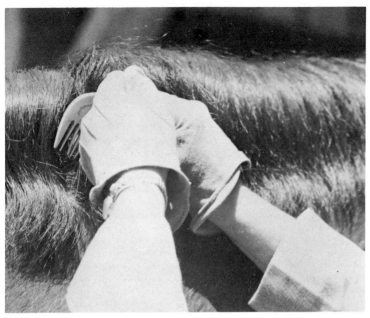

Back comb this section of hair with the mane comb, exposing the full length of the strands in your fingers.

In the hot weather or "fly season" there are several kinds of sprays or wipes that we like to use on our horses after grooming. These wipes can be obtained from the saddle shops and really do keep the flies off for several hours. Using a rag moist with spray or wipe we rub the horse's belly and hindquarters. His head and neck and particularly under his jaw need special attention. These fly control sprays and wipes are not inexpensive but they more than make up in the comfort for the horse and pleasure of his rider.

Take a better grip with your left hand and jerk sharply to pull this hair out.

PULLING THE MANE

If pulling the mane is done quickly most horses will not appear uncomfortable. If you have grasped too many hairs and have to jerk hard, the horse will probably object. Try again with fewer hairs being held. Continue this operation up and down the horse's neck until you have a mane of even length, approximately six inches long. Go slowly at first, step back from the horse as you progress, and watch what you are doing. Please do not use scissors to cut a mane or tail off squarely. Try to keep the natural shape.

Electric clippers are preferred, but a steady hand and a pair of round-tipped scissors can do a good job. Clip the long guard whiskers from around the muzzle and the long hair from under the lower jaw. Remove the hair from the fetlocks. A bridle path, about four to six inches in length, from between the ears can be removed, leaving the fore-lock natural. The hair from the ears may be trimmed by gently folding the ear closed with your hand and trimming downward.

The practice of trimming a horse is just to complete the picture of a neat, well-cared-for animal. This is done regu-larly (every two weeks or so) by persons who are com-peting in horse shows, parades, or any other public event.

With the small electric clippers the ears can be cleaned out, making them completely free of hair. However, this removes all the guard hairs from the inside of the ear and thus permits an easy entrance of foreign matter. Horses that are not just stall horses but are allowed some freedom should not have their ears cleaned out. Twitching or earing the horse is often necessary when trimming the inside of the ear.

Body Clips are done when it is desirable to keep the horse's body free of the long and heavy winter coat. Some people find that it is much easier to keep their horses clean and that the horse will "cool out" much faster after work-ing him when his heavy coat has been removed. When your horse has been clipped you must protect him from the cold with at least one good heavy winter blanket.

CLEANING THE FOOT

Check your horse's feet before riding. Look for rocks or a nail in the frog, and with your hoof pick remove the dirt from the cleft and heel. Proceed in a regular pattern around the horse's legs: left foreleg, left hindleg, right hindleg, right foreleg. Stand close to your horse with your left shoulder against his and slide your left hand down the cannon bone of the left foreleg. Pinch the cannon bone with your thumb and index finger while your left shoulder is pressed against your horse. As you push your horse on his left shoulder you cause him to place more of his weight on to the right foreleg. The pinching of the tendon and cannon bone will cause a slight irritation to the horse, and his weight will shift to the right foreleg. He then should lift his left foreleg. As the foot is lifted grasp the hoof with your right hand. Now change hands holding the hoof firmly in your left hand. Your right hand and hoof pick can now clean the foot. The left hind foot is picked up in much the same manner. Stand with your left shoulder against your horse's left hip. Pass your right hand over the top of the hip and down the left hindleg. Your left shoulder can press against your horse's hip as the thumb and index finger of your right hand pinch the cannon bone and pull forward. As the hoof is lifted, your left hand grasps under the hoof holding it firmly. Your right hand and hoof pick now proceed to clean the foot. On the right side of your horse, reverse the procedure.

A hoof pick should be strong enough to pry loose a rock that may become wedged into the frog of the foot. In muddy weather your pick will have to remove the dry mud from yesterday's ride should you have forgotten to do so at the time.

THE FOOT

1. CANNON BONE
2. FETLOCK JOINT
3. LONG PASTERN
4. PASTERN JOINT
5. SHORT PASTERN
6. COFFIN JOINT
7. NAVICULAR BONE
8. COFFIN BONE

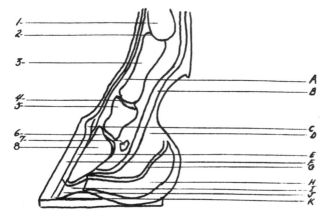

A. EXTENSOR TENDON
B. DEEP FLEXOR TENDON
C. CORONARY BAND
D. PLANTAR CUSHION
E. SENSITIVE LAMINAE
F. HORNY WALL
G. SENSITIVE FROG
H. HORNY FROG
I. SENSITIVE SOLE
J. HORNY SOLE
K. SENSITIVE LAMINAE

For dry cracked hoofs I have found this grease is helpful: 6 ounces glycerine, 6 ounces pine tar, and 1 pound white Vaseline. Mix, apply with a brush around the coronet, walls, heel, and frog for five days, then every third day.

SHOEING

The art of shoeing the horse has been practiced for many years and in many ways. The care of your horse's feet should be put into the hands of a competent horseshoer who will instruct you in the type of shoe your horse requires and how often he should be shod. Follow his recommendations just as you would follow a doctor's instructions and prescriptions. Advice on foot problems can also be suggested by your veterinarian.

The primary reason for shoeing is for the protection of the horse's foot. When the foot is worn away faster than it can grow, it must have the protection of the shoe.

The horse's hoof is like your fingernail and needs about the same type of attention—cutting or trimming to shorten or shape, paring to remove the dead horny structure, and filing or rasping to smooth the rough edges before reshoeing. We find that the need for resetting old shoes or reshoeing will vary with each horse and the amount of work he is doing. Usually six to eight weeks is about all a horse can safely go before the horseshoer is needed.

It is difficult to price the cost of a set of shoes, for some horses will need a variety of types or methods. Types of shoes coming immediately to mind are bar shoes, rolled toes, calked heels, leather pads, and the many ways of adding weights and length to the foot of the saddle bred show horse.

I have noticed that many people when preparing and conditioning their horse for a specific event, possibly a long trail ride, never plan a shoeing program too. The thought seems to be: "I'll have him shod just before or just after the ride." So your horse is shod two or three days before the ride and ends the ride sore or short. There are several minor things that may happen that could cause the condition: excessive rasping on the sole leaving it flat or a nail clinched too tight (or a high nail) causing a shortness of stride. So you wait until after the ride to have your horse shod and your horse is again short in stride. Here again just minor things: a shoe slightly turned, a pulled nail cracking the wall, or the heel of the shoe pressing against the frog.

I have my horses shod at least a week before a specific event and I continue to work the horse after the shoeing. If the horse at this time goes a bit short I have time to ease off of him for a day or so.

Occasionally, in working with horses, it is necessary to perform an operation that requires the horse to stand quietly. This may occur when the horseshoer is working on the horse's feet or the veterinarian is performing a minor surgical treatment. As we have learned, the horse's strength far exceeds our own and therefore methods must be used to give us an advantage over his will to resist. Some methods used are temporarily painful to the horse but do no permanent injury and are applied only as forcefully as necessary to keep the horse still. I do not suggest that you practice these methods but rather understand why it is necessary for the veterinarian or horseshoer and their assistants to do so. The most direct method used is "earing" the horse. The ear is strongly grasped at the base and rotated slightly. If the horse stands quietly no further twisting is required; however if he moves, his ear is twisted more. A "twitch" is a mechanical device consisting basically of a stick with a cotton rope forming a loop attached to one end. The loop is placed over the horse's upper lip and twisted firmly holding the lip. Control is obtained by twisting the stick. In practice, the discomfort experienced by the horse is usually just enough to take his mind off the operation being performed on some other area of his body, and the whole experience is quickly forgotten in much the same manner that we forget a trip to the dentist *after* it is completed. Other methods of control including tranquilizers and sedation can be used by the veterinarian on more serious occasions.

4.

TACK AND EQUIPMENT

The tack room can be any shed, corner, wall or spot where your horse equipment is kept. It can be a very elaborate one with the stable colors, horse pictures, ribbons, and trophies placed all around, or it may be just a plain and simple shed where saddles, bridles, ropes, and halters are kept. Try to keep the room where your tack is kept free from dampness in the winter, as excessive moisture will cause mildew to appear on the tack in a short time. To clean the mildew from your tack is a timely chore that should be done as soon as this condition is discovered. Placing your tack near a furnace or heater will dry it and cause cracking. Tack that has been dried out needs lots of rubbing with a good light oil. Care and saddle soap will help restore your equipment to a long life of usefulness.

Neat's-foot oil or olive oil should be worked well into the leather with your fingers. Use this oil on latigo straps and on all buckles and fastenings where the leather may need extra protection from wear. Do not use any oil on your reins, the seat of your saddle, or the fenders. I suggest just the use of saddle soap here.

A one-horse operation should have the saddle on a rack,

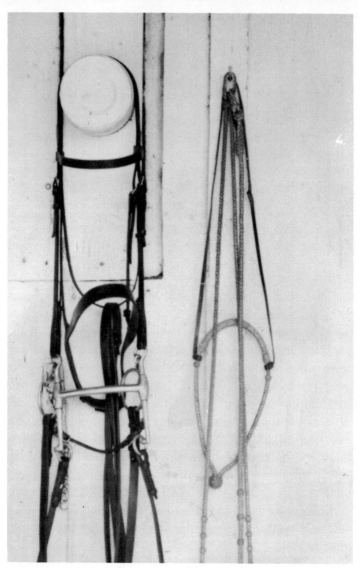

Hang rawhide reins by the loop in the end, using the
weight of the bit to keep the reins straight. Take out
any kinks and curls after hanging. I hang my reins over
a finishing nail. A nail that has a large flat head will
catch the loop on the nail. This continuous wear will require the replacement of the reins sooner than necessary.

the bridle on a coffee can nailed to the wall, brushes in a cardboard box, and first aid medicine (refer to the veterinarian chapter for possible contents) in a closed container. Try to keep this area neat and have your gear where you can find it. Return your equipment, each piece to its proper place, after using. This will take just a minute but can save hours of wasted time looking for lost articles.

Hang your bridle and halter on one-pound coffee cans that have been nailed to the wall. Save the plastic lids and place small items in the cans and cover them. Hoof picks, tooth brushes for cleaning bits, small rags, and pieces of sheep skin are now easy to locate and are out of the way. Hang the bridle by the crown piece, the brow band away from the wall, and the reins down but not touching the floor. I loop the reins back and fasten them in place with the throat latch.

Making a bridle rack from "peg board" is not difficult, and it makes a very handy place to hang many pieces of equipment. A manufactured hanger about two inches in width fits into the board and is a good size to hang the bridles on. The peg board can be nailed at a convenient height on the wall and your hangers placed where you wish.

If you have a Western saddle that is not getting a lot of use and you want it out of the way but still available, you could hang it on the wall. To hang a stock saddle on the wall run a short rope, looped, through the fork and over the saddle horn. Hang the other end of the loop over a strong nail driven securely into a crossbeam.

Oftentimes the transportation of saddles from your home to the stable or pasture where your horse is kept is necessary. In the trunk of a car or the bed of a pick-up truck lay your saddle on its side. The stirrup is flat on the

down side. When laying your saddle in the bed of a
pick-up put your blankets down first. This will save your
saddle from some wearing against the metal bed and will
keep your blankets from blowing away.

In your car the saddle could sit over the back of the
front seat or rest on its pommel in the back seat.

When a saddle is placed down so the tree is spread to
take the weight, extra wear is going into it. In a short
period you will notice the skirts begin to curl upward.
English saddles particularly will not stand much treatment of this sort. The tree in the flat saddle has never
been famous for hard use. When placing saddles on the
ground you could rest them on the pommel for a short
period such as a lunch break.

The grease-can saddle rack can be made from an eight-pound grease can that is available at service stations. The can rests on two crossed 2 x 4's with a 2 x 4 connecting for stability, or it may be bolted to the wall. Add some reinforcement to the end that is fastened to the wall. The saddle rests on top, and all your other gear is placed inside.

Your saddle blankets can be put over a broom handle. Attach the broom handle to the wall with baling wire at each end. You can throw your blanket over the saddle to help keep it clean.

The practice of keeping a sharp knife in the tack room is a good idea. The knife is kept for emergency use only—to cut a rope should your horse get tangled in it. Also keep a pair of wire cutters with the knife.

HALTERS

Halters are made of many materials and will vary in cost, wearing quality, and use. The least expensive and probably the most practical for horse use is the Johnson halter, which is made of cotton rope that when purchased is white. These halters will wear for a long time and retain their strength and utility. Recently, synthetic fiber has been used in making halters and, depending upon the value of the rope, they are usually more expensive. Nylon is stronger than cotton and will not rot or mildew and therefore become weakened by being wet. Polypropoline, while not as strong as nylon, will not mildew but it will stiffen in cold weather and is more subject to abrasion.

A good strong leather halter with brass fittings is more attractive than a rope halter and if cared for in the same manner as your saddle and bridle it will last for a long time. Light-weight leather halters with rolled and stitched parts are appropriate for showing a horse and should be reserved for this purpose, but a more durable halter should be used at home.

Leather lead straps may be referred to as "stud chains." The chain is fastened to pass over or under the horse's nose through the "D" ring in the halter. The strap is held in the right hand. Avoid holding your hand on the chain, for a horse pulling away can hurt your hand as the chain is pulled through.

This lead strap will give you the advantage of more control should your horse be unruly. However, we are of the opinion that horses should be taught manners and the proper way to be led is a very important one.

CARE OF TACK

The care and the cleaning of your equipment is very important. Good leather, when properly cared for, will last a lifetime. Just the daily use of equipment that is in contact with the horse's hide and his sweat will start the process of the loss of flexibility unless wiped clean each day.

A solution that I use to clean dirty tack with is about ¼ cup ammonia to one quart water. Apply this solution vigorously (at least once a week) to remove the old grime before applying saddle soap. Just the application of saddle soap, after several days, will build up a layer of gum-like dirt that should be removed. After each use I like to wipe my bridles and saddles with a clear water rag and then use a light application of glycerin saddle soap. I do not like to dip the bits into a water container to clean them. Often the leather too is submerged and then not thoroughly allowed to dry, followed by an application of saddle soap. This constant dipping of the leather in water without proper drying is the beginning of the loss of life to leather with cracking and stiffness.

BITS

There is no substitute for patient and competent training. No bit, no matter how severe, will replace it. The purpose of the bit is to "cue" the horse to perform your wishes. It is not meant to punish him or force him to obey by pain.

Greater control of the horse may be obtained by increasing the severity of the bit, but there is a limit that is very quickly reached in control and the excessive pain inflicted by the bit only causes hysteria in the horse instead of response to the rider's command.

Before investing in a new cure all bit borrow a similar one and try it on your horse for a day or two to insure that it will accomplish the desired result.

Curb chains are used on the Pelham and on the curb bit of the Bit and Bradoon or often called Double Bridles. These are adjusted so that two fingers can slip between the chain and lower jaw. Twist this curb chain in a counter-clockwise manner to lay flat against the chin. Use a lip strap to hold the chain in place. Curb straps are used on western bits; lip straps may be desired to hold the curb straps in place.

Rawhide thongs are good for handy repair. They will mend broken reins and fasten blanket straps and blanket buckles. They will lace stirrups or boots and are also useful in tieing rolls of clothing together.

There are many types of bits that are designed to accomplish various purposes. The simplest bit is the "snaffle." This bit is probably the most comfortable a horse can carry. If your horse responds readily to a simple and comfortable bit, use it; however, it may be necessary to use a bit with slightly more mechanical advantage. A simple Western bit with moderate cheeks properly used will be almost as comfortable as the snaffle but does give more control. A Pelham bit for English riding is comparable to this Western bit. Be sure that the bridle is adjusted properly on the horse's head so that the bit is in contact with the upper corners of the lip but not pulling or distorting the mouth. Even more discomfort will be experienced by the horse if the bit is low in his mouth, striking his teeth.

HORSE BLANKETS

There are many kinds and sizes of horse blankets. They range from light summer sheets to heavy winter blankets and come in sizes from 68 to 86, measured in inches from the neck opening to the rump. When throwing the blanket on the horse, stand close to his left shoulder facing the rear. Swing the blanket over his back and fasten the front straps. Straighten the blanket at the rear by pulling over the rump, then buckle the belly straps. If you have to blanket your horse with a stiff wind blowing, have the horse face directly into the wind. As the blanket is thrown over the horse it will settle down into place on his back and not over his head.

SADDLE BLANKETS AND PADS

The saddle blanket is used to prevent the horse's back from being chafed by the saddle. This is accomplished by distributing the point of contact between the saddle and the horse over a more uniform area. If too thin a blanket is used the point of contact will be localized and saddle sores may develop. Too thick a blanket will cause the saddle to roll around, increasing its chance of slipping.

When you first saddle your horse always check to see, either mounted or dismounted, that there is at least a finger's clearance from the horse's withers to the pommel or throat of your saddle.

A pommel pad, a small knit pad, may be added over the horse's withers with the English saddle. A double fold or hair pad added with your blanket will raise your Western saddle off of your horse's withers.

Saddle blankets for Western saddles are usually wool

as they are more absorbent and will permit air circulation if they are kept clean. These wool blankets are either closely woven wool material, folded in half with the fold forward over the withers, or the more traditional Navajo blanket, which is considerably more expensive if it is an authentic hand-loomed Indian product.

Various combinations of foam rubber and felted hair pads are also available, which do not provide as much air circulation as a clean wool pad but are quite satisfactory if kept clean and dry when not in use.

The blanket under an English saddle is referred to as a pad or numa. The types of pads are felted hair, sheepskin, foam rubber, quilted cotton stuffed with hair, and jute. Select one that has the thickness and substance to protect your horse's back from the saddle.

The care and cleaning of blankets can be lessened if care is taken to avoid as much contact with the ground, dirt, and stickers as possible.

Wool saddle and horse blankets should be treated just as any wool product. Do not wash your blankets in hot water with a detergent soap. A mild soap specified just for use on wool may be used. Run water on the blanket, loosening the dirt with a brush in a circular motion. Leave the blanket spread evenly over a fence to dry, preferably not in direct sunlight. No matter how carefully we try to wash wool horse blankets they seem to shrink. When buying these blankets it is good to purchase one that is at least a size larger than you need at the time.

BAREBACK PADS

The ready-made bareback pads that can be bought at

the saddle shop are very popular with some riders. These pads are light to handle and keep the horse's sweat from the rider's seat and legs.

Some of these pads are made with a light wooden stirrup, which I feel is very unsafe. These light stirrups almost invite the small foot of a child to slip through. Should the child fall the chance of his foot becoming caught in these light stirrups is great.

5.

SADDLING AND BRIDLING

This is the usual procedure that is followed when preparing for a ride:

1. Have your horse properly haltered and tied up in the area where you will work.
2. Groom your horse.
3. Put on the saddle.
4. Put on the bridle.

When returning from a ride:

1. Put your halter up between the reins around the horse's neck.
2. Unbridle—put the halter on his head.
3. Unsaddle.

This is a very basic pattern that may seem ridiculous to you but there are people who will forget or just overlook Item #2, grooming the horse.

SADDLE UP

Placing the Western saddle on the horse's back can be accomplished in one of two ways: the one-handed "throw" or the two-handed "lift." The one-handed method requires either a short horse or a fairly tall person and a

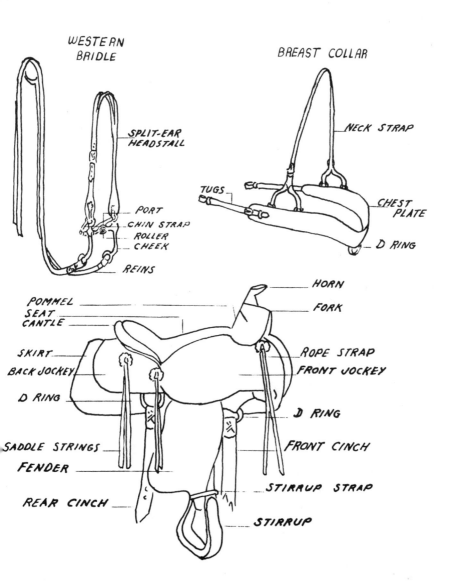

WESTERN
BRIDLE

BREAST COLLAR

SPLIT-EAR
HEADSTALL

NECK STRAP

TUGS

CHEST
PLATE

PORT

CHIN STRAP

ROLLER

CHEEK

D RING

REINS

POMMEL
SEAT
CANTLE

HORN

FORK

SKIRT

BACK JOCKEY

ROPE STRAP

FRONT JOCKEY

D RING

D RING

SADDLE STRINGS

FENDER

FRONT CINCH

REAR CINCH

STIRRUP STRAP

STIRRUP

WESTERN SADDLE

great deal of practice, using a sawhorse or corral rail as the object to be saddled. The saddle is grasped with the right hand through the fork and swung in an arc so that the rigging and stirrup on the "off" side clears the horse's back and then at the top of the arc is permitted to settle lightly on the horse's back. Care should be taken that other people or horses are not in the path of the saddle as it is swung up. This could spoil your swing causing the saddle to fall short of its mark to say nothing

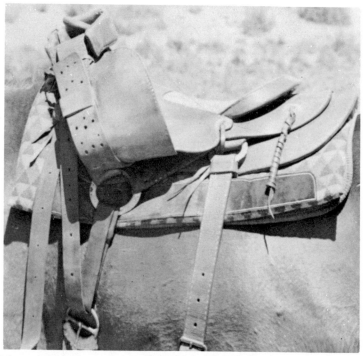

Your left stirrup hooked over the saddle horn will keep it out of the way. I prefer this way instead of tossing the stirrup over the saddle seat, for it can come down striking your hand or head.

To tighten your saddle, pass the latigo strap several times through the cinch ring and saddle "D" ring. Finish with a flat hitch at the "D" ring.

of the injury to bystanders struck in the eye with a flying stirrup.

Many riders find that the two-handed lift is easier to learn, more practical in a congested area, and less likely to frighten the horse. Place the saddle blanket on the horse's back and well forward over the withers. This position will allow you to slide the saddle and blanket back into position smoothing the hair in the proper direction. While the saddle is still on the saddle rack put the cinch across the seat and hook the right stirrup over the saddle horn. Now carry the saddle by the pommel

This is just half the tie completed to the latigo catch. This is not as bulky as the full tie but there is the possibility of its working loose.

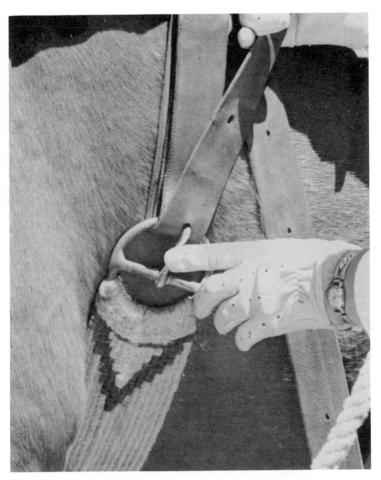

The cinch buckle or cinch ring with a tongue seems to be the easier for me to handle. Instead of the half hitch tie the cinch buckle can be fastened in the holes in the latigo strap. This makes a flat, secure way to finish cinching your horse.

and cantle over to your horse. As you raise the saddle, tip it toward you so that the right skirt will not slide your blankets on over the horse's back. Put your saddle in place and walk around to the right side. Unhook the right stirrup and pull the cinch down in place. Be sure that the blankets are smooth and even under the saddle. If your saddle strings are not tied up check them to be sure that they are not caught under the saddle.

The cinch should hang flat without a twist at the "D" ring in the saddle. The cinch is permanently laced or buckled to the right "D" ring. It will require only minor adjustment when you change from riding a fat horse to a thin one.

A quick check for the proper length of your cinch should be made. The center of the cinch should be in the middle, or right on the center line between the front legs. This will keep the cinch rings from rubbing behind the elbow. Return to the left side and cinch up, but only tight enough to hold the saddle in place while you put the bridle on.

There are some horses that will object quite violently to having the cinch tightened immediately upon saddling. With just the first easy cinching, then bridling and returning to tighten the cinch, you have taken precaution against a "cinch bound" horse.

SELECTING A SADDLE

The procedure of selecting a suitable saddle for yourself is not an easy one. There are so many different types, styles, seats, sizes, and prices to choose from. It is our opinion that good equipment, if it is well cared for, will last just as long as you desire. The future resale of a good used saddle that has been well taken care of is far more lucrative than an inexpensive model that is prone to come apart after some use.

About 30 years ago the style of the Western saddle underwent a change. The high cantle was lowered and rolled and called the "Cheyenne Roll." The seat in the saddle was quilted and the back cinch was added. The back cinch or "double riggin" is intended to hold the saddle in place and prevent it from being pulled forward when a big, heavy calf is roped.

Here are a few items pertaining to the basic size and price of new saddles obtained from our saddle maker. The most inexpensive saddle is $69.50 and is made on an eight-dollar tree that is too narrow to fit the average horse. Your cheap saddle is not much of a saving, for you will soon be riding a sore back horse. For about $600 you can own a flower stamped show saddle. There is quite a stretch in price here, and to start you do not need a show saddle but one that is well made.

A saddle either bought or made for a small child will be on a 12-inch tree. The length of the fender is the main consideration. Fenders are made in three lengths: short, regular, and long. To shorten the stirrup for a small person the fender must be pulled up under the flap. This will make a lump for the child to place his leg over. Fenders can be replaced with latigo leather straps until the child has a chance to grow a bit.

Regular saddle sizes are 14 inch, small; 15 and 16 inch, regular; and 17 inch and more, large. If you have a quilted seat this will reduce the size about one-half inch.

So often a person will purchase a saddle that is too small for him and spend the rest of his riding time sitting on the cantle. Your seat belongs down in the saddle and your back pockets just touching the cantle. The saddle should be six inches wide at the withers and about seven and one-half to eight inches high in the gullet. If by chance your horse is very high in the withers an extra pad can be added with your blankets to carry the saddle properly on his back.

The saddles that we use for our beginning riders have the back cinch removed. Just getting one cinch properly fastened at this stage is quite sufficient. If your saddle has a back cinch, always buckle it after you have cinched your horse. When riding, the back cinch should be in light contact with your horse. Some horses will object to the rear cinch brought tight against their belly at first. If you do need the rear cinch tight, go up a hole at a time. A rear cinch that is hanging four to six inches below the horse's belly can allow the horse to catch his hind foot in it as he kicks at flies.

Always unbuckle your back cinch first when unsaddling your horse. You could forget it and pull your saddle off only to find that now your saddle is hanging under your horse's belly, tied there, with the back cinch around your horse's flank. Your horse will panic at this strange object clinging to his belly and immediately attempt to free himself in the only way that he knows how. In his fright the horse will run and kick at the saddle causing a lot of extra wear and tear. An injury to your horse is very possible, for he will plunge and run, not paying attention to where he is going but only to the object that has caused his fright.

Now that we have just ruined one saddle, a word or two about new saddles. New Western saddles are not made with the stirrups turned but rather hanging parallel to the horse's side, flat with the fender. Each person must

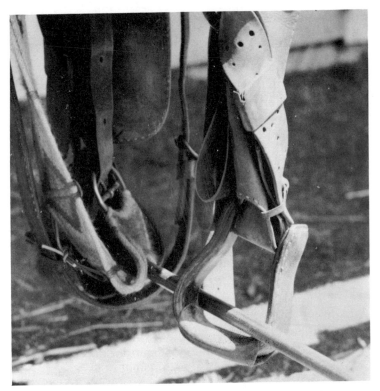

Twist both the stirrups and fenders outward several times. Run a broom handle through both stirrups, tie the handle down and forward. Allow the saddle to dry all day out of direct sunlight.

set his own stirrups. Soaking the stirrups and fenders in a tub of clean water will not hurt or mark the leather but will make them pliable to turn. When the stirrups have soaked about one-half hour, set the saddle on the fence.

When you tie the stirrups down to a lower level board you will pull them into a more forward position, making it easier for your foot to enter. You can tie a bucket full of sand or rocks to the broom handle to hold the set that you wish.

Keeping a broom handle run through the stirrups when not in use will keep newly set stirrups in the desired position. Stirrup fenders hang straight down, a bit forward, on used saddles. Below the fender the stirrup turns out, *not* parallel to the horse's side as the fender hangs.

Stock saddle stirrups whose length adjusts easily, such as those equipped with Blevin and Al Ray buckles, are desirable. Saddle makers can change any laced stirrup leather to a quickly adjustable buckle at a reasonable cost.

PUTTING ON THE BRIDLE

The line sketch of a horse's skull is placed at the beginning of this section for a most specific reason. When an individual begins to learn the art of putting on a horse's bridle one basic panic moment does occur.

Even the most trusted instructor will always raise the hair on the nape of the student's neck by stating, "Just place your finger in the horse's mouth, on the bar, and he will accept the bit." This statement will immediately raise a doubt. Horses are "hay burners," they have long, strong teeth, and so many to fit along that pointed jaw.

Looking at the sketch you will realize that there is a place provided for your finger. The right bar is the spot where your index finger can press down in perfect safety.

The following method of bridling we much prefer. There are several other ways but I believe this way to be the most satisfactory and the easiest to teach and to learn.

Your right hand presses the left ear forward easily

SKULL AND TEETH

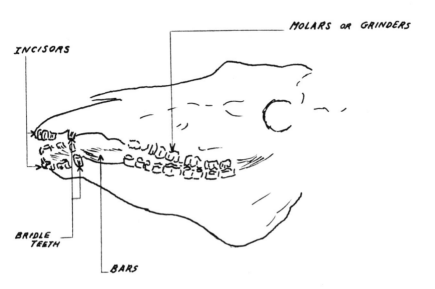

MOLARS or GRINDERS

INCISORS

BRIDLE TEETH

BARS

under the crown piece. Reach over the horse's head and press the right ear forward as you push the crown back to rest behind the ears. Now check your bridle for fit. Is the eye clear and not covered by the cheek piece on the right side? The bit should rest easily on the bars just breaking the corner of the mouth. If your horse keeps throwing his head, possibly the bit is too low in the mouth and is striking his teeth.

Bridles are adjusted to fit by raising or lowering the cheek pieces at the buckles. Some bridles adjust in the crown piece.

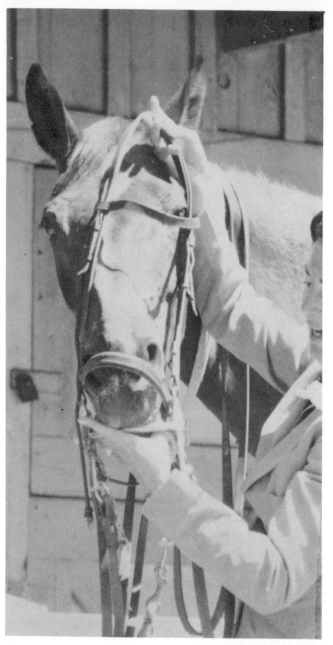

Work on the left side of your horse's head. The halter is on the horse's head. First remove it and refasten it around his neck. Slip the bridle reins over his ears, laying them on his neck. Hold the crown piece in your right hand while the left thumb and index finger hold the bit.

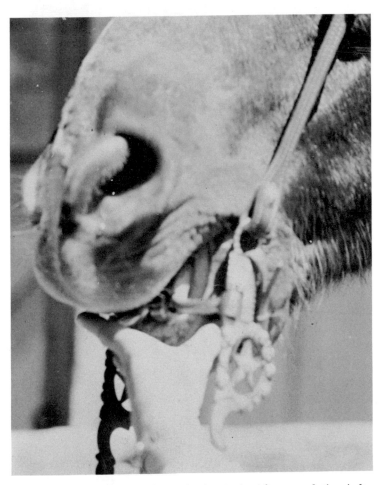

Open the horse's mouth with the index finger of the left hand pressed onto the right bar. In so doing you are letting your horse know that you want him to open his mouth. This method is far superior to a crack on the front teeth with the steel bit, which is guaranteed to create a reaction that in a short period of time will make him impossible to bridle.

After the horse has opened his mouth, raise your right hand and bring the bit into the mouth. Hold it there by pulling upward gently with the right hand.

Now change hands, maintaining the upward pressure with the left thumb.

TAKING OFF THE BRIDLE

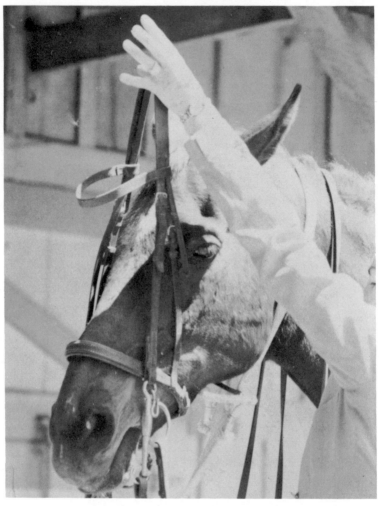

Work on the left side of your horse's head. Run the halter and rope up between the reins and fasten the halter around the horse's neck. Bring the reins forward to the crown piece. With your left thumb behind the left ear gently push forward. As the horse's ears clean the crown piece hold the bridle . . .

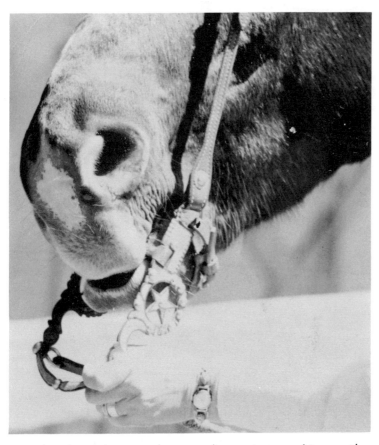

. . . thereby giving your horse a chance to open his mouth and release the bit. DO NOT jerk the bridle from your horse's head, thereby cracking his lower teeth sharply with the bit. Slip your bridle onto your left shoulder, put the halter on the horse's head, start to unsaddle.

There is the possibility that your horse may be very anxious to go to his corral when returning from a ride. As you prepare to remove the bridle, first be sure that you run the halter UP BETWEEN the reins, and fasten it around his neck. Both the halter and bridle reins are now around the horse's neck. Slip the bridle off his head on to your left arm. Unfasten the halter and immediately put it on your horse's head, then bring the bridle reins over his ears. In this way you still have the minimum amount of control with the halter or bridle reins at all times.

UNSADDLING

Work on the left side of your horse. First hook the left stirrup over the saddle horn, unbuckle the rear cinch "double riggin," then undo the latigo strap. Double the latigo strap back through the "D" ring in your saddle. Walk around to the right side. Run the "rope strap" through both cinch rings and slip the strap over the saddle horn or tie the cinch ring to the pommel of your saddle with the saddle strings. Return to the left side and pull the saddle toward you. Lift the saddle to clear its weight from across the horse's withers. With the "riggin" tied to the saddle it will not drag in the dirt or be walked on. Resaddling is easier for the "riggin" is partly out of the way.

A WORD TO THE WISE

In the first half of this book I have tried to touch upon some important points pertaining to your horse. I started at the horse's head and his halter and then examined leading and tying, stabling and feeding, general care, tack and equipment, and saddling and bridling. Now your first adventure on your horse's back can begin. I do not mean to cast a shadow of despair on a wonderful event but mishaps can and do happen. Many times common horse sense is just overcome by the excitement and your enthusiasm.

When you started to work around your horse you put the halter on his head. With his lead rope you have safety tied him to the barn or fence with a slip knot. After grooming your horse, combing his mane and tail and cleaning his feet, you go to the tack room, returning with your saddle and bridle. When you get to your horse, *pull the knot loose* before placing the saddle on his back. A well-broke horse will stand with his rope tossed over the fence as you proceed. Cinch up easily, then remove the halter from his head and refasten it around his neck. Now bridle your horse. During this time should your horse "pull back" you have saved the fence, halter, and rope from breaking. When working around a horse you, or something else, might accidentally startle him into "pulling back" (away) from you. When you are holding the bridle rein or lead rope and the horse does go back, release your hold. Now the tug of war between your hand and the horse's head will end, the contest is over.

At this part of instruction we are using just one rope to tie up the horse. Cross-ties are good and used in many stables, but we have not referred to their use here.

When you are working on your horse, washing or trimming, you may need the assistance of a partner to hold him still for the necessary attention. Both of you work on the same side and do not allow your helper to stand *directly* in front of the horse. Your assistant could be on the opposite side holding the lead rope, his arm and hand stiff against the horse. This will not move the horse on to you but will push your assistant away from the horse should he step in his direction. The horse can go forward but will be less likely to step on either person as he proceeds.

Riding bareback with just the halter on your horse's head can be lots of fun. It can be quite exciting when there are two people aboard the horse. The fellow in back begins to lose his balance and will cling tighter to the first rider, thus sending both people off balance. The first rider now will pull harder on the halter rope. He gets little or no response from the horse to slow or stop him. Just the rope and halter lend very little assistance in the control of your horse, and he will continue on as both riders end up on the ground in a pile.

The great idea of borrowing your friend's horse to go for a ride could be your undoing. Because you don't know his certain moods and mannerisms or his fears and reactions, he is almost a stranger to you. To succeed with horses and people you must first get acquainted with each other. Jumping on to just any horse's back to go for a ride is not like getting into an automobile for the same purpose.

Long pants and boots are worn to help protect you from the wear and tear of the activity in which you are now engaged. Moccasins are permissible, I guess, when riding bareback, but never when your foot will be placed in the stirrup. The soft flat sole and no heel of moccasins or tennis shoes just offer the opportunity for the foot to slide through the stirrup. Boots are made to protect your feet both in the stirrup and on the ground. Having a toe stepped on by a horse is a painful experience suffered by many. It may not seem so at the time but your boot will have helped to prevent a more serious injury to your toe.

Riding with a group of friends will add hours of enjoyment to this fine outdoor sport. When it is necessary to follow one behind the other on a narrow trail keep at least four feet from your horse's head to the tail of the one in front. This will allow your horse to see where he will place his feet and prevent him from stepping on the heels of the horse ahead of him. Horses can hurt horses as well as people when they step on each other. The horse's reaction is to kick at the offender.

When riding along you could get a touch of nausea or dizziness from something that you ate, or even the heat.

Stop for awhile, dismount, and give yourself a chance to feel better while sitting on the ground. It may even be necessary for someone else to go for help if it is needed. Don't keep riding on and on thinking that you'll recover. There is the chance that you could faint or even blackout for a moment and slip from your horse before anyone can help you. In the era when travel on horseback was the only way to get about, one had to keep going. Nowadays modern machines can go just about anywhere that help is needed and they do so in an expedient manner.

MOUNT UP

Having carefully checked your saddle and bridle for its proper adjustment you are ready to mount your horse. This should be accomplished quietly, quickly, and safely. If your leg is short and the horse is tall this makes the task more difficult. To even up the difference reduce the horse's height by placing him downhill from your position or increase your height by standing on a sturdy platform.

There are many ways and styles to clamber aboard your horse but there are two accepted methods.

Mounting One-Half Facing the Rear. Stand with your left shoulder against the horse's left shoulder and take up your reins in your left hand. The reins should be evenly stretched, with a light contact on the horse's mouth. Now get a good handful of mane in your left hand. Your right hand will turn the left stirrup forward to put your left foot in. Hop on your right foot propelling yourself upward. Grasp the horn or pommel with your right hand. Hop up swinging your right leg over the horse's back and sit down lightly in your saddle.

Mounting One-Half Facing Front. Stand with your

right shoulder against the left side of your saddle. Pick up your reins in your right hand and take a good hold of the horn or the pommel of your saddle. The reins should be evenly stretched with a light contact on the horse's mouth.

By placing your left foot in the stirrup, steadying yourself with your hand on the horn or pommel of the saddle, propel yourself upward by hopping from your right leg to a sufficient height permitting you to shift your weight to the left foot. With your left hand grasp a handful of mane. From this position the right leg can be lifted over the horse's back and come to a sitting position. The key to this movement is keeping your weight and center of balance over your left foot. In walking upstairs or climbing a ladder it is impossible to ascend unless you move forward over the foot on the stairs or rung. This is also true of mounting a horse. The hands and arms are used to steady yourself not to pull yourself up. Attempting to pull yourself up by grasping the saddle or reins will probably result in turning the saddle or jerking on the reins, making the horse back or attempt to get away, which complicates the problem even more. Practice stepping up on a box from the ground with the height of the top of the box midpoint between your knee and waist. Gradually increase this height and practice until you can smoothly push yourself up with one hop from your right leg to a standing position on the box.

Mounting in this manner does not present the opportunity for the novice rider to pull on the cantle of the saddle. The English saddle is not strong enough, and the tree may break from this continuous strain on the cantle. The Western saddle can be pulled crooked on the horse's back with this method.

When mounting I find it steadying to have my left knee come in contact with the saddle. This seems to give a good base of support. With your left foot firmly in the stirrup and your left knee in the knee roll the flight upward is a more controlled effort.

When you have become as proficient as possible in this exercise you will find that mounting a horse can be done more smoothly; however, do not be ashamed of using the aid of a hillside or a convenient box. You will find that the most capable jockeys in the world have to be given a "leg" by an assistant or trainer because the distance from the ground to the stirrup is too far for any other method.

You may wish to assist your friend in mounting his horse by "legging him up." You can cup your hands while bending forward. As your friend places his left foot in your hands straighten up and push upward. He must keep his left knee stiff and you must be standing next to his horse. The true "leg up" is just a bit different. Stand next to the horse at the girth area. Your friend will bend his left leg, allowing you to place both hands on his shin. As you straighten up he should spring, using his knee to assist in the upward motion. A word of caution: too much push from you can cause the rider to flip right on over the horse's back.

TWO METHODS OF LEADING THE HORSE WITH THE REINS

Step forward, not looking at your horse. If you have the reins tied to the saddle horn or placed under the stirrup irons your horse cannot be led forward because you have created a back and forward pull at once.

When dismounting, your rawhide reins should not be slipped over the saddle horn but laid around from right to left with the romal hanging down on the left side.

Tied reins should be unknotted before dismounting,

laying the right rein around the horn and holding the left rein in your hand.

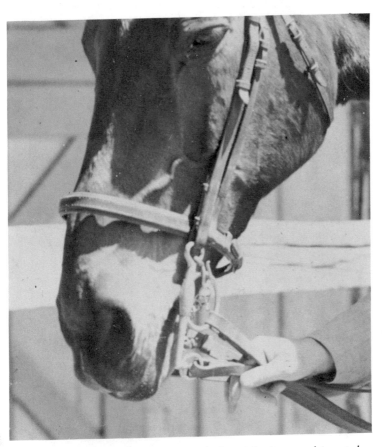

1. The reins are over the horse's head laying on his neck. Stand on the left side at your horse's head. Your right hand grasps both reins just behind the bit with your index finger separating the reins. By holding the reins close to the bit, should your horse wish a playful nip, he cannot reach your hand as easily.

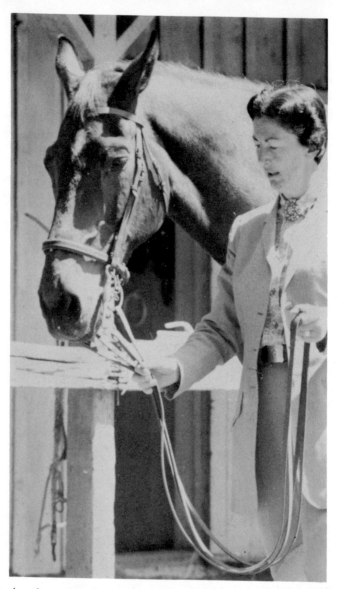

2. In the second method, the reins are over the horse's head. Your right hand grasps both reins just behind the bit with your index finger separating the reins. The romal or extra length is held in, not wrapped around, your left hand. Step forward not looking at your horse. These methods of leading your horse are correct for both English or Western equipment.

LEADING FROM HORSEBACK

Keep the rope of the led horse short, and his head at your right knee. Have both of the horses move as a team at the same speed and gait. If the led horse drops back slow your saddle horse down to prevent the horses from kicking or changing sides. Be alert to what you are doing for you now control twice as much horse power.

When removing jackets or sweaters take your time and preferably dismount. Roll the jacket tightly and tie it behind the cantle with the saddle strings. Roll the left side smaller so that when you are mounting your right leg will clear the roll. Do not ride with your rope strap hooked over the saddle to make a loop, and unless you really are going out to work cattle or drag logs, do not carry a coiled rope on your saddle. These are two more things to get caught up in, should your horse turn quickly to the left and send you off over his right shoulder.

SPURS

Spurs are designed to do a specific job. Until you know just what you wish to achieve with a pair of spurs, it is best not to wear them. If you do wear spurs have them fit your boot and choose a very modest rowel, for it is the manner in which spurs are used that make them effective—not the size of the rowel.

6.

ENGLISH RIDING

When you carry your English saddle and bridle to your horse, do so in a workmanlike manner. Your bridle—the reins too—are on your left shoulder, your saddle is on your left arm with the stirrup irons run up, and the girth is across the seat of the saddle from right to left.

The girth could be doubled in the right side with the fold up through the stirrup iron. The stirrup leather is passed through the girth fold from front to rear to secure it in place. In either case the girth cannot get caught under the saddle or hit you in the face as you raise the saddle to your horse's back.

When you lift your saddle up raise it high enough to clear the horse's withers. This can also be accomplished by tilting the saddle toward you, which will permit the right skirt to clear the withers.

Bridling was explained in detail in the previous chapter. The English bridle has a brow band and a nose band or a cavesson. After you have put the bridle on, check the brow band to be sure that it is straight across the horse's forehead. The right side many times will be pinching the right ear as the left side almost covers the left eye. Adjust the cavesson to rest straight across the horse's nose

ENGLISH BRIDLES

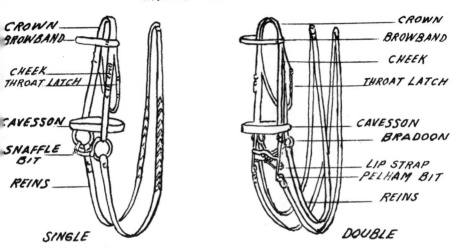

CROWN
BROWBAND
CHEEK
THROAT LATCH
CAVESSON
SNAFFLE BIT
REINS

SINGLE

CROWN
BROWBAND
CHEEK
THROAT LATCH
CAVESSON
BRADOON
LIP STRAP
PELHAM BIT
REINS

DOUBLE

ENGLISH SADDLE

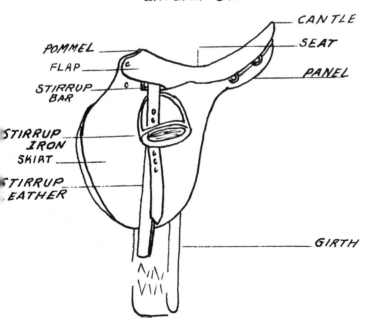

POMMEL
FLAP
STIRRUP BAR
STIRRUP IRON
SKIRT
STIRRUP LEATHER

CANTLE
SEAT
PANEL

GIRTH

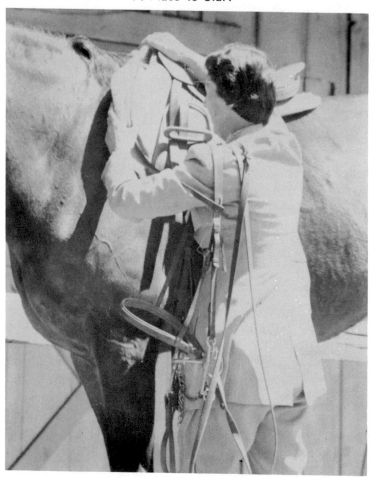

Put the saddle far enough forward on the withers so you can slide it back into place. Avoid pushing the saddle forward and possibly turning the hair on the horse's back. This may cause a sore or tender spot. After putting your saddle on the horse's back, walk around to the right side. Be sure that the pad is flat and the girth is not twisted. Return to the left side and tighten the girth just enough to hold the saddle in place while you put the bridle on.

and make certain the cheek pieces are not covering one eye.

Keepers are on a bridle for a purpose; use them. They should be slipped up and over the ends of the adjusting tabs. Nothing presents a more sloppy appearance than riding along with the end tabs of the cheek pieces waving in the breeze. When the keepers are kept in place the end strap or tab will not curl up but will always lay flat against the cheek piece.

Before mounting you should always check the girth, which must be tight enough to hold your saddle in place while you mount. If adjustment is necessary—and it should be, for you did not tighten the girth at first saddling—slip your left arm through the reins, to have minimum control of your horse, and proceed to tighten your girth with your right hand.

The saddle will have three billet straps, but most girths have only two buckles. I fasten the first and third billet possibly with the idea that the saddle is more evenly balanced.

STIRRUP LENGTH

When mounted you can again check the stirrup length. While sitting in the front of your saddle with a comfortable bend in your knee slip your feet out of the stirrups. The stirrup iron should be even with your ankle bone. For more advanced cross-country riding and jumping it should be a hole shorter. This again is just an approximate check.

Changing the stirrup length while sitting in the saddle will only be helpful to you if you are sitting in the correct place. There should be at least a hand's width between your buttocks and the back ridge of the cantle. This will put you in balance with your horse or "with the horse's center of gravity."

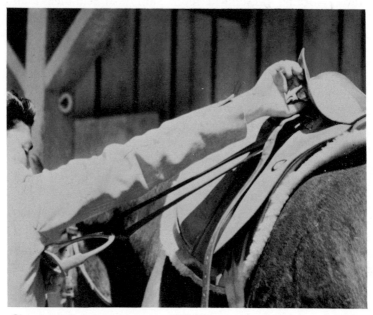

Check your stirrup length. Standing at the left side of your horse, place your right thumb knuckle on the stirrup buckle. Hold the tread of the stirrup with your left hand to your right armpit. The stirrup leather should be just stretched. This is an approximate length but it is a rather good check.

Changing your stirrup length while mounted can be done quickly and easily. There is nothing quite as exasperating for a whole group to have to wait while someone stops to adjust his stirrups. You should practice this and be able to make stirrup changes at a trot and canter.

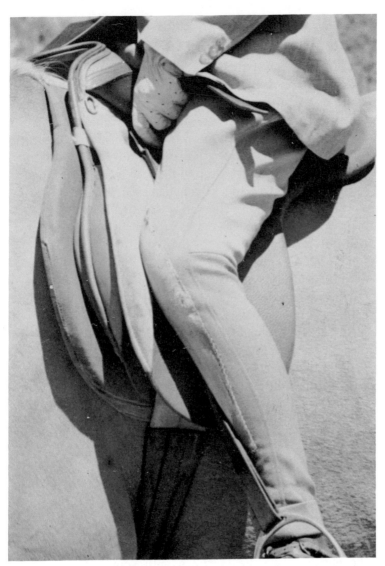

Adjusting your stirrup length while mounted. Left stirrup, left hand. Your foot remains in the stirrup. The knuckles of your left hand are forward, your thumb and index finger are on the stirrup buckle. To change the length of the stirrup, lighten your weight in the iron without removing your foot and pull up to loosen the buckle. Your thumb and index finger move the tongue of the buckle to the desired hole in the stirrup leather. Return the buckle against the stirrup bar by pushing down on the inside stirrup leather with your left hand. Right stirrup, right hand.

Check the safety catches of the stirrup bar. These catches are movable hinges that the saddle maker has made in the stirrup bar. The catch is intended to release the stirrup leather from the saddle if the rider should fall and catch his foot in the iron. When not checked, these hinges will become frozen, possibly in the closed position. With your fingers and a drop of light oil work these hinges so that they are free and will change easily from the closed to the open position. The safety catches can always remain open, for if the leg is in its proper position the stirrup will not come off.

The tread of the iron is carried on the ball of the foot with the leather laying flat against your shin. If the leather is twisted remove your foot from the iron and rotate the leather to remove the twist.

Stirrup irons should be large and heavy. Your foot is placed on the inside of the iron with about an inch of width from your little toe to the outside curve. Riding with small, light irons can prevent you from getting your foot out of the stirrup quickly if the need should arise, and always wear a hard leather-sole boot or shoe that has a heel.

CHECKING THE GIRTH—MOUNTED

After you have mounted check your girth again for tightness. The girth need not be so tight that it will cut the horse in two. Reach down with your left hand and slip two fingers comfortably between the horse and girth. If it is too loose you can easily tighten your girth as you walk along. Sit erect in your saddle and hold your reins in your right hand.

With a double fold girth the fold is always forward, i.e., the opening or raw edge toward the hindquarters. Having

Keep your left foot in the stirrup and carry your left leg forward past the skirt of the saddle. Raise the skirt of your saddle over your thigh and hold it with the thumb and index finger of your right hand. With your left hand, reach for the billets. Your knuckles are forward and as you pull up the buckle will release. Your index finger will select the next hole in the billet strap.

the raw edge just behind the horse's elbow could cause soreness from rubbing as the horse travels along.

DISMOUNT—TWO WAYS

Step Down. Take your reins in your right hand. Have them evenly stretched with light contact on the horse's mouth. Place your right hand firmly on the pommel of your saddle and your left hand on the crest or mane. Take your time and be sure that your right foot is completely out of the iron before you swing your right leg over the horse's rump. Your balance is now transferred to your hands. Your right foot will touch the ground and you can then remove your left foot from the stirrup. The secret here is the balance on your hands and your left knee against the saddle as you step down. A child or short person will have trouble dismounting in this manner.

Slide Down. We have our children slide down on their stomachs. Your reins are held in the same manner as the *Step Down.* Remove your right foot from the iron and swing your right leg over your horse's rump. Place your weight on both hands and take your left foot out of the stirrup. Now slide to the ground. The trouble here is that belt buckles will skin up the saddle leather as the rider slides down on his stomach.

In either way of dismounting the reins are not used to assist. If your balance is lost, recovery will be far less disastrous if the reins are dropped.

As you prepare to dismount take your time and think of what you are going to do. First, be sure to free your right foot of the right stirrup iron. Take your foot out of

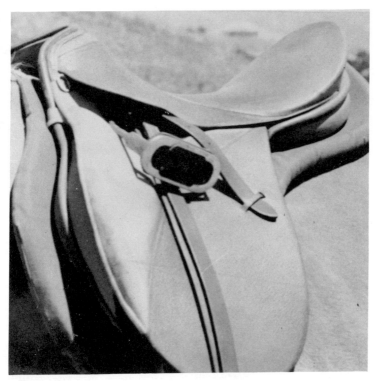

When dismounted, always have the stirrup irons run up on the inside stirrup leather. By getting in the habit of running your stirrup irons up to the buckle you are avoiding the possibility of an accident with your horse. Horses have been known to reach for an itch on their barrel and catch the stirrup iron over their lower jaw. When a horse finds himself caught in this manner the result can be disastrous, both to the horse and any others in the immediate area.

If you do not intend to unsaddle your horse immediately, tie the stirrup leather back through the stirrup iron. You can secure the iron close to the stirrup buckle with a half hitch at the top of the iron with the stirrup leather. This tie will also shorten the length of the stirrup leather. Your stirrups are tied securely to the stirrup buckle and are out of the range should your horse reach for his side to bite a fly.

the stirrup and let it hang for just a moment before swinging your right leg up and over the horse's rump.

When you dismount by sliding or stepping down, be certain that you are not pulling on the reins to assist you. If you slide down from your saddle, remove your left foot from the left stirrup before slipping down from your horse. If you step down, get your left foot out of the left stirrup quickly while you still are in balance next to your horse.

RUN UP YOUR STIRRUPS

By securing the stirrups in place with the half hitch in the leather, you have taken the best precaution against a possible accident. Should your horse shake himself or even get loose and run, the stirrup irons are tied up and will stay up out of the way.

UNSADDLING

Unbridling was explained in detail in a previous chapter but reminders are always good.

First: Bring your halter up between the reins and fasten it around the horse's neck behind his ears and unbuckle the throat latch.

Second: Left hand—left thumb, bring the reins to the crown piece.

Third: Left hand—left thumb—left ear, slip the crown piece and reins forward over the ears.

Fourth: Hold the bridle and allow your horse to open his mouth to release the bit.

Fifth: Place the bridle on your left shoulder, refasten the halter on your horse's head and tie him.

Step to your saddle. With the stirrup irons previously run up, the skirt of the saddle can be raised to unbuckle the billet straps. Lift your saddle high enough to clear the withers and slide it toward you, and your left arm passes under the pommel to hold the weight of the saddle. With your right hand catch the girth and place it on the seat of the saddle.

Your bridle is on your left shoulder, and the saddle is carried on your left arm. This is a very efficient way to get the job of unsaddling accomplished.

Your horse can now have his saddle mark brushed off and he can be returned quietly to his stall or corral.

SPURS

Spurs should be worn high on the heel of your boot. When the spur has been allowed to hang at the bottom of the heel, its use is rather ineffective. When the spur is high, just the rotation of your calf to the rear will bring the spur into contact with the horse's side. A low-hanging spur requires the action of the whole leg and foot to make contact. Use spurs tactfully and correctly.

The buckle of your spur is fastened on the outside of each boot. If the spur buckle is in the middle or inside of the boot there is a possibility of its catching on the stirrup iron.

NEW SADDLES

If it is possible, before purchasing a new forward seat saddle try to ride several different types and makes. The "flat" English saddle is made in standard sizes from 12 to 18. The size is determined in inches measured from the cantle to the button in the flap. The length of your stirrup leather should place your knee comfortably into the knee roll.

A suede knee roll may make the variance of ¼ inch in size. The Italian-made saddles can change in exact size, as these craftsmen are working with centimeters from an order placed in metric inches.

There are saddles made just for the type of riding that you may prefer: polo, dressage, saddle seat, or just a good comfortable hack saddle. Some saddle shops will allow you to try the saddle before purchasing it. A new saddle should fit both you and your horse. When you are allowed to try a new saddle take precautions against soiling or marking the leather. The stirrup leathers should be wrapped with a clean cotton bandage, which will prevent marking the saddle skirt with a leather mark.

7.

TRAIL RIDING

Trail riding and good manners with consideration for others are one and the same. Unless a designated "race track" has been constructed in your riding country there is no rhyme or reason to be running your horses. Running horses in an area where other unsuspecting riders may be violates all sense of reason. The same rule applies to horses as well as to automobiles: "the faster the speed the more control necessary." However, very few individuals practice this theory.

When overtaking riders slow down; if they are having trouble controlling their horses, hold back. Don't go barging ahead scattering riders and horses all over the country. When passing, walk quietly by; don't stop and allow your horse to sniff noses with each new fellow he meets. Many colds, coughs, and flu are passed along this way. When you are ahead again, start off slowly, at a jog, or slow trot, giving the rider in the rear a chance to hold his horse back without dashing madly down the trail.

When crossing a stream or a bridge give your horse a chance to examine this obstacle for himself. He may be smarter than you in not wanting to cross a bad mud bog or a bridge with loose boards. However, if you have examined the situation and find it safe, continue to urge your horse patiently to move forward; if your patience outlasts the horse's resistance you will have accomplished your purpose. At any rate, be prepared for a long engagement. Applying excessive force will result in an excessive resistance with either your horse or yourself suffering probable injury. Even if the obstacle is negotiated while the horse is near panic, little has been accomplished because the act cannot be repeated unless the same force is applied.

A good "rule of thumb" to follow is: if the way ahead does not look too good and you have to go on, get off and lead your horse.

If your horse pants for air half way up a long hill let him stand, facing away from the prevailing wind, catch his breath for three or four minutes, and then proceed. If the hill is very steep, quarter up it—zig and zag. Get your weight off of your horse's loins, lean forward. Proceed in this manner by holding on to the saddle horn or his mane with one hand. The bridle rein is light allowing the horse full use of his head and neck as he climbs.

Walk down hill. On a long downgrade have a light steady hand on the bridle rein. Encourage your horse to walk along, straight down the hill. At a sharp down drop or bank, encourage your horse. Have an easy hold on the reins. Quarter down, let your weight drop to the rear. Give your horse a chance to find his way without much disturbance from you. Going down hill in a great rush may seem like fun, but this procedure can very quickly turn into a complete disaster as your horse can trip, resulting in all somersaulting toward the bottom in a big pile.

When you are riding on a narrow trail, such as up a hill with the down side on your right, you may have to turn around. A good way to do this is to stop your horse and let him stand quietly for a moment. Turn him so his head will be in the direction of the down slope and he can see where he is going. If he needs more room to complete the turn he can back against the hill. Allow the horse freedom of his head and to make his own adjustments to the situation as he sees it. Sit still and encourage him to be quiet and slow as he maneuvers in a narrow place.

Today so much of our riding country is criss-crossed with paved roads of one type or another. Here are a few precautions you may want to take to heart. When riding along a paved road stay on the dirt shoulder and face the oncoming traffic. If you are traveling north be on the left shoulder with the southbound cars passing to your right. Look ahead, there could be a large truck approaching. He will be traveling relatively slow so you might have a moment to select a wide spot to be in as the truck passes. Keep your reins up and your horse's mind on his business. A sudden backfire or blowout from the passing traffic may cause him to veer away.

CROSSING PAVEMENT

When you wish to cross the pavement check to be sure that the road is free of automobiles in *both* directions. Also, look at the pavement, and avoid crossing where a lot of oil has been spilled or a tree has created shade and moisture has dripped down from the foliage. Such spots will be very slick and cause a horse to slip quite easily. Now ride straight across to the opposite shoulder.

If there are several riders, three or four or more, all turn as one and cross in a flanking movement. All horses arrive on the opposite side at once and traffic is not delayed as one at a time marches by. Equestrians and pedestrians have the right of way; however, do not trust the driver of an automobile to look out for you.

When we do so much of our riding in part or whole along a roadside, cars and horses sometimes have a bit of a problem. The uppermost thought is that "the rider must be aware of the automobile." Even on a quiet back road, auto drivers act as though they never in the world would expect to see a horse and rider. The driver of the automobile dashes everywhere as though he were on an expressway.

The rider must be aware of these modern drivers. He must keep his mind and the horse's mind strictly on business when riding on roadways.

Don't let your horse just wander along. He may be just a foot from the shoulder strip but in many cases this can be just enough to cause an accident.

HIKERS, BIKERS, PIPE LINES

The trails that we are allowed to ride on are often thoroughfares for other interests, people, or things. When overtaking or meeting pedestrians, ask politely if they would stop for a moment and step to the side of the trail as you pass. Walk quietly by and say thank you. When the group that you come upon is a gathering of small boys with long hiking sticks, shouting and waving all together, your guess for the safety of all is as good as mine.

Bike riders always seem to have trouble getting their bikes clear of the trail but will usually try to do so. However, it always happens, one or more bikes will fall over just as you pass. This will cause an immediate flurry as the bike owner tries to drag his possession back to safety. Nevertheless, say thank you and proceed on with unruffled feathers.

Motorbike riders may be a bit of a problem. They may give you the right of way, but the puffing of their machines often may create some difficulty. But be appreciative and proceed as possible.

Never walk on an exposed pipeline, as it may be very slippery. Old pipe could be rotten and break when a horse steps on it.

TIE-UP ON THE TRAIL

If you plan a picnic you have brought lunch for yourself, so plan for your horse, too. You will want to tie up your horse while you eat so take along his halter and tie rope. You may want to leave the halter on your horse's head, and by slipping the bridle on over it the halter rope can be looped around the horse's neck or tied to the saddle. Keep an eye on your rope, for if it does work loose you can retie it before it drops under the horse's feet.

WATERING ON THE TRAIL

In some areas this can become a problem. If you have watered your horse well, letting him have his fill before leaving on the ride in the morning, he is in no danger of

If you have planned well you can tie your horse quite safely. Look for a tree with a strong limb about four feet above the ground or a strong V in the tree about "horse head" high. Clear away sharp, strong branches and small protruding limbs. Provide room for the horse to move his head without danger of poking an eye. Use a slip knot with enough length so that the horse can move about but cannot get a foot caught in the rope.

When you have tied your horse, stay around, watch him, don't go off leaving him alone. There might be a possibility of your walking home if you are not around to prevent or stop trouble when it develops. When you have tied your horse loosen the cinch just a hole or two. The saddle should not be so loose that it might slip under the horse's back. Don't forget to reset your saddle and tighten your cinch before mounting.

becoming too thirsty. If you should cross running water, such as a stream, let your horse drink here if he wishes. Don't let him paw or play too long in the stream, for some horses will take advantage of this chance to roll in the water.

Public watering troughs and tubs where all may drink might pass along colds and coughs.

Leave all gates as you find them. If the gate is closed when you get there, go through the gate and close it. You have been granted the privilege of riding through someone else's property—protect this trust. Open all gates to their fullest. If it is a swinging gate, fasten it open before leading the horse through. Wire gates should be pulled back, parallel to the fence line. By pulling the wire gate against the fence line you avoid the possibility of a horse catching a foot in it as he passes through the opening. A horse could become frightened and whirl, plunging into the wire gate that has been left lying on the ground. If you must ride through a narrow gate, do it slowly, guide your horse steadily and easily, and get your knees up out of the way.

If your friend has dismounted to open the gate, accept this courtesy by riding through the opening and then wait for the other person to mount his horse. When a rider continues on, not waiting for the one who still must mount, he will place that dismounted person in a very dangerous position. The horse that is to be mounted will be anxious to join the one that has gone ahead. The rider now must mount alone, but on a horse that probably will not stand still. This is an almost impossible situation and one that can—and often does—place the rider in a very bad spot.

When you are on the ground helping a friend to mount his horse that will not stand still, get yourself in the position where you can be of assistance. Step to the left shoulder of the horse and take hold of the bridle by the left cheek piece with your left hand. You can assist by holding the left knee of the rider with your right hand or by giving a boost to the rider with your right hand. Your left hand is holding the horse so he can be turned in a left-handed circle around you.

When assisting from the back of your horse, have the horse to be mounted on your right. Take hold of the bridle at the left cheek piece in your right hand, holding the horse's head at your knee. Swing your horse's hindquarters off to the left allowing more room for the rider to mount. Hold on to the other horse until his rider is secure and in a position to take control. I like to hold the bridle by the cheek piece and have the rider hold the reins. The rider now has the full use of his reins to control his own horse. You are just assisting in this control by holding the horse's head without having to transfer the reins from holder to rider.

When riding again, if the other horse continues in his restless mood, hold your horse back. With your horse slightly in the rear you will give the other rider a better chance to settle his horse.

POSTURE

After you have been on your horse's back for several hours you may begin to get weary. Now that you are getting tired you will tend to lose your correct seat and balance. Maintain your good erect posture. Do not slouch and flop in your saddle. Your horse could be getting tired too. When you slouch and sit with all your weight on one side your horse has a double job. Not only must he keep on carrying the initial weight but in your efforts to become more comfortable you add weight to the wrong places. A better procedure is to dismount and walk for a period of time. This will relax your sore muscles and give your horse a rest.

Before remounting change your stirrup length a hole in either direction; this will change your position enough to vary the previous stress. Sometimes after a period of riding you may experience a sharp pain (a muscle spasm in the diaphragm) just below the rib cage, which can be alleviated by inhaling deeply for a minute or two. The same procedure can be followed if you are unlucky enough to be thrown from the horse and land on the ground, which will "knock the wind out of you." The foregoing will be of no use until you have experienced the sensation, but you will recognize the situation when it occurs.

OVERHEATING YOUR HORSE

When returning from a ride avoid coming back to the barn area with a "red hot" horse.

If you plan your ride so that your horse returns to the

stable in a cool, dry, and calm condition you may proceed to unsaddle him. You can just brush off the dry sweat and maybe give him a chance to roll. He may drink his fill and be returned to his stall or corral.

A hot horse, however, must be walked cool. Some people prefer to remain on the horse as they walk, while others find that a horse will "cool out" faster by hand walking. Allow this horse just a swallow or two of water every few minutes. Do not let him drink his fill immediately, for this is the easiest way to make him sick. After walking your horse dry, brush away all the dried sweat. In about an hour, if you are lucky, you may return him to his corral.

There will be times when a horse will be overheated from some specific work or training session. Horses that are in training for the show ring—for example hunters, jumpers, stock and cutting horses—will work hard and get very hot. The trainers or owners who get their horses in this overheated condition also know how to properly and carefully cool them out. The method of allowing the horse to walk slowly in a circle around you is good. We call it "gyping," which permits the horse to relax and "cool out" while saving you many steps. You can teach your horse this way with a bit of patience and perseverance. It is best explained as a triangle, with you at the apex and the horse forming the long side. To have the horse move to your left push his head away from you and encourage him to step forward. A small stick in your right hand may keep him going. Keep increasing the length of the lead shank until your circle is about ten feet in diameter. Remain at the center of the triangle unless the horse slows down. To encourage your horse step forward more to your right or his left rear. With a little practice you can soon have your horse walking quietly in the circle around you.

8.

HORSE SHOW

Horse shows are for the participation of the exhibitors and the entertainment of the spectators. At a show you and your horse are the entertainers so it is important to put on a good show. Have your clothes neat and pressed, your boots polished, and your tack clean (freshly soaped leather, polished bit and buckles). Your horse should be at his best, his coat brushed and shining and his mane and tail brushed or braided. Your good attitude and manners will especially be on display so do credit to yourself—win, lose, or draw.

There are many kinds of shows that you are eligible to participate in:

  a. Play Days. Usually some horse show classes and some gymkhana (games) events are scheduled. The prizes are small ribbons, with sacks of feed, grooming equipment, halters, or levis for the winners.

  b. Schooling Shows. Primarily to give actual ring experience to young riders and/or young horses. Usually ribbons and small trophies are given to the winners.

  c. Local Shows. Usually will attract just local exhibitors. Prizes can be ribbons and small trophies.

111

d. Point Shows. These shows will attract many exhibitors who are competing for points toward the yearly championship and reserve championships offered by the different Horsemen's Associations. The association that is offering points at that particular show will be clearly listed on the entry form.

GOING TO A PLAY DAY

Let us assume that you have heard that the local Junior Riding Group will hold a play day. Contact one of the club members to find out who you may call to get all the information. The details are printed on the form known as a classification list or entry blank. The events planned for the day, at what times they will be held, and the amount of entry fee to be charged for each class will be listed.

Check the list of events and enter the ones that you and your horse are qualified for. If you want to enter the Trail Horse Class, you had best practice a few more times. Open gates and let your horse see some typical obstacles that you might encounter in the ring.

Fill out the entry blank and be sure to have your parents sign in the place provided. Mail or take your blank to the show secretary before the day of the show. You may find that post entries will be accepted. This means that you do not have to enter before the day of the show. You may enter on the show grounds with the entry clerk when you arrive. If the class or classes that you wish to enter are to be held at 1 P.M., plan to arrive in plenty of time. When riding over to a play day, take your horse's halter and tie rope, for you may wish to tie him while you have a bite to eat. Carry a water bucket with a brush or two in it so that you can water your horse and clean him up after the ride to the show.

When you arrive, tie your horse away from a crowded area and check in with the entry clerk. If you have entered ahead of time there will be a number waiting for you; if not, the clerk will give you a number when you enter. Numbers are worn on your arm or back, so please display your number properly. Find out how soon your event will be held and be at the back gate in time.

If you have to wait for your class, or are just hanging around the show to watch for fun, act like you belong. Don't go racing your horse up and down, raising more dust and generally making it unbearable for the people who really want to watch the proceedings. When you are just sitting on your horse, sit as though you were a rider. Sitting sideways, backwards, or with a leg hooked over the horn doesn't prove a thing. After all, the show is in the ring and if you do have some talent, why not display it to the judge. You might get a ribbon for your efforts.

It is your responsibility to be ready for your class. Do not expect to be called. Arrive in the immediate area at the back gate at least while the class ahead of you is going on. When your class is called the gate will be opened by an attendant. Sometimes these people are checking the contestants' numbers as they enter the arena. Be courteous and proceed into the ring in an orderly manner without pressing ahead. The usual gait when entering will be the jog or normal trot. You will be instructed if there is a change.

PROCEDURE IN THE SHOW RING

The gaits that you will be asked for in the show ring

are the three natural gaits of the horse—the walk, the trot, and the gallop—but with modification.

The walk can be broken down into slow, normal, and extended.

The trot will be the slow or sitting trot for the English division. The Western division has a slow trot, called a jog, which is also a sitting trot. The normal trot, not usually asked for in the Western division, is the posting trot for the English division. For the extended trot, used in both divisions, you can sit, or raise up in your stirrups.

The gallop for the show ring or trail riding is slow and collected. This will be the lope in the Western division or a canter for the English division. The gallop is the extension with more speed and lots of control. The extended gallop or full run is for the race track only. When the judge of the show wishes the extended lope or canter the announcer will instruct the class. He will ask you to "extend the lope" or "extend the canter" or "gallop on."

When riding in the ring your line of travel will be about three feet from the rail (fence). The line on which you are traveling is called the *track*. When traveling with your *left* shoulder toward the center of the arena, you are *tracking left*. Riding on or at the rail is the same as riding on the track. When *tracking right* (right shoulder to center) to *reverse,* turn your horse smoothly to the right (away from the rail) about six to eight feet (½ circle). Return to the track at the same gait in the opposite direction. When passing always pass toward the inside of the ring, never between another horse and the rail. Be considerate and leave enough clearance to avoid cutting off the other rider at the rail. When passing another horse coming from the opposite direction always pass left shoulder to left shoulder.

To extend your gait move your horse along rapidly, maintaining the original gait. *Hold hard—halt—stop.* Immediately hold your horse in place stopping straight on the line of travel. After you have traveled both ways in the ring you will be asked to "line up." You will be instructed as to the direction to face the line. Enter the line from the rear. Allow room on either side and don't push your horse into the line right on top of the horses already standing. Don't stand in the line with your knee squashed onto the rider next to you. Leave room between the horses should the judge wish to pass between. Look at the line-up and stand your horse evenly with the others. If you are asked to "back" your horse, do so quietly, without a jerk on the reins. Pull your horse straight back for just a few steps, and then move forward to the original line.

After the judge has finished checking his card the awards will be made. If you are a prize winner ride forward and receive your ribbon with a smile. A gentleman will ride forward and remove his hat as he smiles and says "thank you." When you are among the many that do not receive a prize, ride easily and pleasantly out of the gate. Possibly this was not your day, but keep practicing and you will succeed.

SUGGESTED PROPER CLOTHING

Suggested Western clothing to wear to a show. Always be neat and clean.

a. Long-sleeved shirt.
b. Boys—Western choker or small string tie.
   Girls—Small tie or pin at the collar.
c. Straw or felt hat that fits snugly. Stuff the brim with

kleenex if it is too large. Use hair spray on the hatband or your forehead. Girls can use an elastic band under the hair. Your hat is worn straight across the eyebrows, not tipped back on your head. Wear your hat when riding at home. Get used to wearing it and perfect the art of keeping it on your head. Hats that suddenly come flying off will cause quite a bit of excitement to unsuspecting horses and riders.

d. Girls, your long hair must be covered with a net or tied in a bun, *not* flowing on your shoulders.

e. Gloves, if worn, are natural in color, not colored or sparkling.

f. Clean levis, frontier pants, or equitation pants.

g. Leggins or shotguns, but have them fit you. Better none at all than a poor fit. Avoid wearing chaps in an Equitation Class for chaps do not show clearly just what position your leg may be in.

h. Boots should be clean and polished, free from dust and dirt.

i. Spurs are optional, but if you wear them, make sure they fit.

If you choose to wear gloves, have your own pair. A pair too small will give your hand a very odd appearance. A pair that is too large can get caught in buckles or chains.

Also have your own shotguns or leggins. The fit is most important. When spurs are worn, leave the leggins unfastened about six inches from the bottom to prevent your spurs from forcing the leg up.

Here is a suggested list of clothing to wear when showing in the English Division of a horse show. Here too, is more than needed for a play day. Have your clothing neat and clean. Do not appear in clothing that looks like it has been slept in.

a. Long-sleeved shirt.

b. Bow or four-in-hand tie for boys.
Colored choker or pin at the throat for girls.

c. Hunt cap, black or colored to match the coat.

d. Girls, your hair must be neatly in a net or bun but *not* flowing on your shoulders.

e. Coat, black or colored. Several years ago it became quite the style to have the hunt cap and coat of the same color. This outfit was worn by Junior riders in Equitation, Pleasure, and Road Hack Class. Instead of staying with the modest shades and colors some riders began to appear dressed in colors for a circus event. This was immediately frowned upon and discontinued. If you intend to show in a large show and are not certain just what to wear, your black cap and coat will always be correct.

f. Breeches, yellow or tan; jodhpurs, yellow or tan.

g. Boots, black or tan, or jodhpur shoes, black or tan. Have them polished and free of dirt or dust.

h. Spurs are optional, but if worn, make sure they fit you and the event.

i. Gloves, leather or string.

NEW CLOTHING FOR YOU

So often your parents will buy that new pair of boots you have been wishing for just before a show. It is very nice to have a new pair of boots to show in, but they are not broken in and very uncomfortable, particularly at the ankle joint. The leather soles are smooth and will slip in the stirrups. After you have put up with the discomfort of stiff boots and slippery soles all day, your horse show will be an unhappy event. Any item of new clothing you buy—pants, coats, hats, yes even a stock tie—should be purchased much before the specific time to wear it.

Hunt caps are worn squarely on your head, straight above your eyebrows and parallel to the ground. As you progress in the English division you may want to try the Hunter or Jumper events. In all classes in which the horse is required to jump, the riders must wear protective headgear. Crash helmets and hard hats were made to protect your head, so fasten the chin strap.

Now that you have been to a play day and I have listed the clothing that is worn at a horse show, maybe you too will be bitten by the "bug." Before you go on, know that there are basic rules for all sports, including the horse show.

The American Horse Shows Association, 527 Madison Avenue, New York, N.Y. 10022, is the governing body of all horse shows. Any one starting to show should know and understand the rules of his division, which are all clearly written and explained in the yearly rule book published by the AHSA.

You can join the American Horse Shows Association with a Junior Membership Fee of $5.00 per year, or a Senior Membership Fee of $10.00, and with either one you will obtain the rule book. Here are just some short notes on the further progress of horse shows. If you have aspirations of eventually showing in the large shows that are held around the country, you must be prepared to spend a great deal of time, money, and effort. Your AHSA rule book will also tell you in detail the proper dress and tack to be used for each division.

Local Shows—Enter on the blank enclosed with the prize list and/or classification sent by the management of the show. Read the list of classes offered and understand the specifications of each class. Enter only those that you and your horse are qualified for, and know what will be required of you.

County or State Fairs—Premium books list both a section and the classes to be held in that section. Be sure to include both numbers when entering. Do not send your horse's registration papers, just his registration number shown on his papers. Keep your papers available but safe. Replacing lost papers can be long and costly. Where the weight of your horse is required, your veterinarian could give you quite a close estimate to put down on the blank.

Recognized Shows—This show is licensed and recognized and rated A, B, or C point show by the AHSA. The management has paid a fee, and thereby must comply with all the complete specifications of a AHSA show. It must follow all the rules and regulations specified in the AHSA rule book and must have licensed personnel, a steward, and a judge (or judges). Any discrepancies here are settled by the Board of Directors of the AHSA.

HALTER CLASSES

Showing your horse in Halter Classes can be a lot of fun. Before you enter this event do a little planning and work at home. The time that you have spent will be rewarding, for you will have a well-mannered horse for the judge to inspect at the fair. When you lead your horse into the ring, two things should be considered: How well your horse will show and how well you will show your horse.

A good halter horse will be very well mannered, stand quietly, and move willingly at a walk and trot. The exhibitor will be attentive, quiet, and alert, and he will keep on showing his horse until the class is dismissed. At home teach your horse to stand, lead, and halt.

This is one way to prepare your halter horse. Stand square, face your horse (standing directly in front of him) with your lead rope in your right hand. Hold the horse straight, notice his feet are placed evenly. If he steps forward tap him on the nose and say "whoa." A horse that is standing square could also be said to be standing with a "leg at each corner." Your horse has a large body that is supported by even distribution of his weight over the four legs. The legs are in a natural position, not too close together, front to rear, for this will give your horse a "bunched" look; too far to the rear gives him an elongated look. Have the horse at a natural stance, with all four feet doing their even share of supporting each quarter. You can move your horse's back feet by using your halter rope to push his head back and your hand to move him over. By swinging the horse's head to the left or right you can encourage him to step forward to bring his front feet even with each other. Do these exercises quietly and notice what you are accomplishing.

Here are a few of the classes that are offered when your horse will be shown on the halter. There are one or two classes when some exhibitors prefer to show with a bridle suitable to the division.

1. Child's Model Mount
2. Model Stock Horses
3. Model Hunters
4. Both sex and age groups for all registered breeds—Quarter Horses, Appaloosa Horses, Arabians, etc.
5. Junior Showmanship

When leading your horse work on the left side at the head. The lead rope or strap is in your right hand, about two feet from your hand to the halter. The extra length of rope is in your left hand. Step forward and do not look at your horse. For an unknown reason, a horse will not be led by an individual who is "staring him in the eye." Encourage your horse to walk and jog at your right side. You may need some assistance from a friend behind the horse when you first start leading. You will find it necessary to turn your horse while leading him. To make a right turn without your horse pushing into you, your right elbow used against his left shoulder will help to turn him away. When moving the horse, travel on a straight line and make sure that when you turn you will return to the original line of travel.

Stop—halt. Do not look at your horse. Stand facing the front. If your horse will not stop when you do, a sharp snap on the halter rope as you say "whoa" may help. Stop and stand on your line of direction, both you and your horse facing forward.

After you have shown your horse, move back into the line, stand your horse evenly, and keep his attention until the class is dismissed. Show your registered horse in the classes provided for them, avoid putting registered horses in grade classes.

Registered horses are horses produced from duly registered and recorded parents. All registered animals have papers giving their registration number and the names of all the past registered parents in their line. When purchasing a registered horse, be sure that you have the correct papers for this animal. The sale should not be completed until these papers are properly filled in by the seller. Any responsible dealer will provide you with the proper registration papers in good order at the time of the sale. Beware of other transactions.

Grade horses are horses produced from a registered stallion out of an unregistered mare. When purchasing a horse bred this way attempt to obtain grade horse papers on your animal.

When you are going to a show take your own bucket of water and your own grooming equipment. Water your horse from his own bucket. Colds and other diseases are transmitted by letting your horse drink from any container other than his own. Use your own grooming equipment too, for it is possible to pass skin disorders from horse to horse as the brushes go around.

THE DAY BEFORE

The day before the show is always a very busy one. If your horse is in good show condition he should be first worked as usual and then polished for the show. To try and mention every item of grooming and finishing that is done for each different breed and each specific division would be impossible. Here are some of the basic preparatory steps we do for our horses the day before.

We show quite regularly so our horses are kept trimmed. If your horse needs to be trimmed again do this first before you get him wet. We have a bridle path cut between the ears and on to the crest about four to five inches toward the withers. The whiskers and lower jaw are clipped. The ears we just fold together and we then remove the long hairs that will extend from the fold. Our horses are out quite a bit so we do not remove all the small guard hairs from the inner ear. The fetlocks and coronet band are trimmed. We do not clip the manes and tails but keep them pulled.

Some people give the horse a complete bath, shampoo, and rinse before each show. Of course if your horse is a light color—gray, white, pinto, palomino, or buckskin—a bath before each show is almost a must. White legs or feet are always washed and cornstarch is rubbed in while the legs are drying. This is brushed off when dry and more can be added the next morning if necessary.

The solid-color horses we like to wipe with baby oil. With the oil on a rag, rub the horse's coat and around his eyes and nose, also the hocks and front legs. This will put a shine on the coat, which should be rubbed well again the next morning. We also rub the entire horse with fly wipe on the morning of the show. With the palms of your hands rub firmly and see the coat shine.

While the tail is still wet we wrap it in a bandage to lay the hair smooth and straight against the tail bone.

If the mane is unruly and will not lay down wrap a gunny sack over the mane around the horse's neck. Allow the mane to dry in this manner and often the hair will stay in its proper place. Your hunter or English equitation horse may have his mane braided the day before the show but not his tail.

To do a good job on tail braids the hair must be pulled tight. I do not like to have a horse stand all night and then all day at the show with his tail done up. We have found this to be a direct cause of cranky, switch-tailed hunters. With practice you can learn to braid a tail in less than 15 minutes on the morning of the show. *Please* take the braid *out* of your horse's tail as soon as you are through showing him. If you have a three-hour ride home in the trailer, or longer, and then because you are tired you wait until the next day to unbraid the tail, you are not being very considerate of the horse that has worked hard for you.

Now pack all the things together that you will take with your horse in the morning. I have heard of people arriving at the show without their saddle. Running around trying to borrow equipment from others at the show is very embarrassing and difficult.

Before leaving for the show there will be a few things to do. Repair a braid or two in the mane, polish or grease the hoofs, and maybe add a little more cornstarch to the white legs.

Leave early enough so you do not have to rush and tear around. Haul your horse quietly in his trailer. Plan so that you both arrive relaxed and ready to enjoy your show.

9.

TRANSPORTATION

If you are thinking of possibly attending a horse show or a trail ride out of your immediate area, you must consider the problem of horse transportation. It seems that this matter can be easily solved by simply putting your horse in a trailer, attaching this trailer to an automobile, and away you go. However, there is really more here than meets the eye.

First, is your car or truck heavy enough to control the weight of approximately an additional 2,000 pounds of live weight pushing it downhill? Does it have the power to pull this additional weight up a long hill?

Second, your local motor vehicle code specifies the proper hook up for brakes and lights. Remember to check these requirements before going very far.

Third, the hitch itself should be made properly for the car or truck. An agency that sells trucks and trailers, a custom truck shop, or blacksmith shop that builds trailer hitches may be able to help you. These shops may also be able to adjust the brakes and lights for your equipment.

Fourth, is the trailer large and strong enough for the horse or horses that will be put in it? Some horses haul better with just a dividing bar in the center of the trailer.

A solid center board is sometimes desirable, but it does help to have this factor solved before going very far down the road. Check the manger for places to tie your horse. Is the tie ring in the front or at the side and does the partition that separates the horse's head come far enough to the rear to prevent the horse from turning his head before being tied in front?

Fifth, now that you have complied with all the motor vehicle code regulations—and your outfit is satisfactorily equipped with all the necessary safety features—will your horse get into the trailer? The whole plan can break down right here. If possible, try to work with your horse a few days in advance of the planned trailer ride. Patience and fortitude will be your best guides here. There are many people with this problem; some have solved it one way, others another, but remember a horse that has been hurt or badly scared in a trailer has very good reasons for not wanting to go into it again. It is a very long and difficult process to successfully reclaim a badly spoiled horse that some careless individual has thoughtlessly scared or hurt in or around a trailer. A horse that loads and rides well is a joy to have and a great credit to your ability when it comes right down to the final test.

To include here all the many ways and means of hauling or transporting horses from one place to another would be impossible. Here are a few ways that we use and have found quite successful.

Our trailers are the tandem axle, full top commercially built type. These trailers are the two- and four-horse models with the dividing bars. We like the single bar divider instead of the solid panel between our horses. They seem to ride better when they have that extra space to step over.

Our trailers are either the step in design or have the tail gate ramp. The hollow sound created when the horse steps on the ramp may cause doubt to your horse. Give him a little time to get used to the new noise and conditions.

The inside of the trailer has the single divider bar with the solid head partition. This head divider extends about four feet to the rear, just about to the horse's withers. This long extension will prevent the horse from turning his head when entering the trailer. The solid head divider seems to keep the horses from trying to nip at each other.

There are two or four strong tail chains that are fastened after the horses are loaded. These chains are about three and one-half feet above the floorboards and are bolted to the side of the trailer. A large metal snap secures the chain to the dividing bar. Be sure these chains are fastened so the divider doesn't slap against the horse's sides while in transit. Tail or butt chains will assist in preventing the horse from backing out of the trailer before you desire.

The manger has a permanent chain fastened in it. This chain is about two and one-half feet in length, just long enough to allow some freedom of the head to eat. We fasten the horse's head with this chain, not for security but to make a separation between the lead rope and the permanent chain. The horses ride with the lead rope tossed over their necks, but on a long haul the ropes are unfastened and just the chains are used. Some people prefer not to leave the lead ropes on their horses when they are in the trailer. We leave it on, for if you have to unload in a hurry the rope is always available on the horse.

The front of the mangers are padded to prevent the

horses from banging their knees if a sudden stop is necessary. We have a rubber mat on the floor, which seems to give the horses better footing and prevents slipping on the moist floorboards.

When preparing to load our horses we put feed in all the mangers. Hay or meal will give the horse something to do as he travels along.

We load by "sending" the horses into the trailer alone. Do not get into the trailer with your horse for there just isn't room for you both. When you are loading into the large vans someone must be inside to place the horses into their stalls.

This method of "sending" the horse into the trailer with the lead rope tossed over his neck has been taught to all of our horses. We work with our horses to teach them this way and it saves hours of time and energy.

When the horse enters the trailer the tail chains are fastened and the halter is secured to the chain in the manger. We use the rope halters on the horses when hauling because they are stronger than the leather halters and more inexpensive to replace when broken. The tail gate is closed and fastened securely. The ramp tail gate should be lifted by the side only. Standing directly behind the ramp to lift it is very dangerous, and the horse can step back and push the ramp down on you.

Now that the horses are loaded and standing quietly eating, we start off *slowly*. Give the horse a chance to find his balance with the motion. We live by the rule: "If you hear the horses moving in the trailer, *slow down*." A horse that has always been given a chance to get his balance and stand easily in the trailer will always haul well. You may note that nothing has been said about wrapping the horse's legs. If the horses are hauled properly there is no reason for wraps or boots. Horses will not deliberately step on themselves. It is driving that will cause any disaster. If you start off at a flying pace, pull around corners, and slam on the brakes, the poor horse has no chance at all of survival.

There are many excellent types of shipping boots and protective equipment for your horse available at saddle shops. These I would not hesitate to purchase and use should it be necessary for others to haul my horse.

When we arrive at our destination it may not be necessary to unload all the horses immediately. The required horses are unloaded and tied to the trailer or van; the others stand quietly eating and relaxed. When we unload from the trailer, first the halter chain is unsnapped. Then the tail gate is opened and the tail chain is unsnapped. This is accomplished without standing *directly* behind the horses but by reaching across from the side.

The trailers have a dome light and a light in the front tack compartment. These lights have separate ON and OFF switches that save time fumbling around in the darkness. These lights make it much easier to work around the horses if an emergency should occur in darkness. Standard equipment on the trailers are running and direction lights and brakes—a requirement in many states.

To quote a price on a trailer is difficult. The many manufacturers of good quality trailers and horse vans will be delighted to help you make a selection.

Some people prefer to build their own equipment while others wish to see the completed product.

Trailers are built in the one-, two-, or three-horse capacity. The four-horse van that will attach into the bed of a pickup truck is very handy for some. A choice of the width of the body and height to the top is available. The large deluxe horse vans that will ship six to 12 horses are in demand by large stables and commercial lines.

The transportation of our modern, pleasure, show, and race horses has really taken a giant step forward.

10.

VETERINARY CARE

When moving into a new area that you are not acquainted with, for your horse's sake locate a veterinarian who handles large animals. Your telephone directory will help with the names and numbers of those who are in practice. A phone call at the time, saying who you are, the type of horse that you have, and where you keep this horse will save some valuable time when the need for a veterinarian arises. It is a good idea to have his phone number written down and kept in a safe place by the phone for an emergency.

Some of the common ailments referred to in this section I have described with visual symptoms only. The treatment and the administration of any medication has been purposely omitted. I feel strongly that the novice horseman should not attempt to treat the sick animal. The point here pertains to the fact that a little bit of knowledge may be disastrous to the recipient.

If an accurate record of the animal's temperature is kept and the visual signs of distress are determined, your veterinarian can make a correct diagnosis.

Rectal thermometer. When your horse is obviously not feeling well, start to take his temperature twice a day, if possible. When you call your veterinarian it will help him determine more readily the immediate need for his services.

The internal temperature of your horse is determined by the insertion of the thermometer into the rectum. The mercury is shaken down and the bulb lubricated (white Vaseline is good) and inserted into the rectum where it is left for two or three minutes. The normal temperature of the adult horse is 99.8 to 101 degrees F. It will be higher in the evening than the morning and will raise after meals and exercise. A mild fever is about 102.5 F., a moderate fever about 104.5, and a high fever above this. The natural constrictions of the rectum can envelope the thermometer. We fasten a string to the end of the thermometer with adhesive tape. The string can be wound into the tail hairs for the period of insertion.

Antiseptic solution. For washing and cleaning cuts and abrasions, use Phisohex surgical soap, Hydrogen Peroxide three percent, or just plain soap.

Antiseptic powder. For washing and cleaning cuts and abrasions when cuts or wounds are moist and need drying up.

BFI Powder can be purchased in the drug store.

McKillips Dusting Powder.

Sulpha-Urea Powder.

Bandages. Flannel strips about four inches wide and about six feet in length and roll or sheet cotton to use beneath the bandage.

Please do not make quilted pads to use in place of

sheet cotton. This quilted padding, usually made from cup up bed pads, will slip and twist under the outer bandage. When the tried and true method of using three sheets of cotton and the flannel wrap are used your horse will have the protection and help he will need from a bandage.

Colic: A horse that has a stomach ache—for basically that is what colic is—will do several things. He may lay down, roll, get right up, then lie down again. He may kick at his belly with his hind legs, bite at his side and flank, and paw heavily on the ground. These are not the normal actions of a healthy horse so do not confine this horse in a small area or stall. Watch him quietly, keep him moving, and prevent him from rolling near or under a fence.

While the horse is in distress he may wish to lay down, particularly if he has been in pain for some time. Allow the horse to be quiet if he wishes to rest. It is the violent rolling and thrashing about that may cause further internal trouble. If the animal will stand or lay quietly you can let him do so. If he persists in rolling you should keep him on his feet, moving easily until your veterinarian arrives.

If you go to the horse, be careful, for in his efforts to relieve his distress he may injure you.

Lameness: All horses move at a true cadence beat. Get accustomed to this rhythm and count it when you are riding. Walk, four beat; trot, two beat; lope or canter, three beat. Notice the natural gesture of your horse's head and neck as he travels along. However, when the hoof beats are not true and the head is making more of a down-ward (lower) gesture as the one forefoot strikes the ground, it is a pretty good bet that you have a lame horse. Dismount and look for a rock or nail in his foot, check him for cuts or injury. If there are no outward causes showing, call your veterinarian.

Coughs, Colds: Horses seem to show the same signs of a cold as you do. Your horse may appear listless and refuse to eat or drink his usual quantity. He will cough quite frequently, have more discharge from his nostrils, and run an above normal temperature. This you would only observe if you had been using a rectal thermometer. Do not ride your horse at this time. Watch your horse, and if he doesn't seem to be definitely getting better in just a few days, call your veterinarian. A cough or cold can easily develop into pneumonia.

Heat and Swelling on the Back: When removing the saddle, especially after a long ride in the heat, check your horse's back. Run your hand, palm down, lightly over the back in the direction of the hair growth, head to tail. Note any swelling or tender spots.

Swelling may be reduced by rubbing the horse's back with a strong circular motion from the palm of your hand. This will help to reduce the swelling from heat and fric-tion of the saddle blanket. I have used a salt-water solu-tion of four tablespoons of salt to one quart of cool water. Sponge on the back for heat and tenderness. Do not ride a horse with a sore back. Whenever your horse is not well or hurt and sore do not ask him to work for you. Give him a chance to heal before you demand service from him.

Bleeding from a Wound: If your horse has been cut (usually from barbed wire) and there seems to be profuse bleeding, the application of a pressure bandage may be used. This can be done by making a pad out of several folds of sheet cotton or some flannel material, such as your old winter pjs or a diaper, and place it over the wound. Sprinkle some antiseptic powder on the wound, and then on the pad and wrap the strips of flannel firmly. Do not tie by making strings out of the end of the bandage. This type of fastening could cause more trouble than you are already in. Fasten with large safety pins. Diaper pins can also be used to hold your bandage. The use of the common Ace bandage for horses is absolutely *out*. An Ace bandage, when wrapped around a leg, will tighten with movement. A person can loosen the tight bandage but a horse is the victim of a well-meaning soul. As the bandage tightens, the circulation of blood is stopped and many other complications might arise.

INDEX